Developing
your
Organisation

Alan Lawrie

Published by
The Directory of Social Change
24 Stephenson Way
London NW1 2DP
Tel: 020 7209 5151, fax: 020 7209 5049
e-mail: info@dsc.org.uk
from whom further copies and a full publications list are available.

The Directory of Social Change is a Registered Charity no. 800517

ISBN 1 900360 66 7

British Library Cataloguing in Publication Data
A catalogue record for this book is available from the British Library

Cover design by Lenn Darroux
Designed and typeset by Sarah Nicholson
Printed and bound by Page Bros., Norwich

Other Directory of Social Change departments in London:
Courses and Conferences tel: 020 7209 4949
Charity Centre tel: 020 7209 1015
Research tel: 020 7209 4422
Finance and Administration tel: 020 7209 0902

Directory of Social Change Northern Office:
Federation House, Hope Street, Liverpool L1 9BW
Courses and Conferences tel: 0151 708 0117
Research tel: 0151 708 0136

CONTENTS

ACKNOWLEDGEMENTS

Organisations are complex and ever-changing bodies. This book aims to help people working in the not-for-profit sector understand and improve the effectiveness of their organisation.

This book is based on the issues, problems and ideas developed in my consultancy work. I am therefore grateful to the individuals who allowed me to pick their brains, test the material in the book and review their experience.

I am grateful to the publishing staff at the Directory of Social Change for their support, to Bill Mellor for his comments on the text and to Jan for helpful comments and advice throughout.

Alan Lawrie
March 2000

We would like to thank Kogan Page Limited for granting permission to reproduce the transition grid on page 89 from their title, Managing Organisational Change, Scott and Jaffe, 1989. Although every effort has been made to trace the copyright owners, we have have been unable to contact them. If they wish to contact the publishers we would be pleased to hear from them.

This publication is kindly supported by NatWest.

About the author
Alan Lawrie is an independent management consultant who works with public sector and voluntary agencies on management, organisational and strategic development issues.

INTRODUCTION

This book aims to help managers, board members and staff of not for profit agencies build and develop their organisation. It concentrates on problems commonly faced by voluntary organisations and has the following three themes running through it:

Responding to external change

Organisations cannot stand still. The rate of external change is fast. Organisations have to respond to new demands, new expectations and new requirements and staying the same is rarely an option. Organisations have to find new strategies, new structures and new ways of organising.

Finding new ways to work

There has been considerable debate recently about how best to organise and manage. Some of these new ways of thinking are only temporary fashions whilst others are more sustainable and can make the organisation more effective.

Managing organisational change and development

Organisations are always developing, so they need to find new ways of managing change to ensure that the organisation continues to grow, develop and respond.

This book is structured in seven chapters:

The first chapter looks at organisational development and helps you to review the issues facing your organisation.

Chapter 2 looks at developing, planning and implementing strategy. This chapter outlines a process for formulating a strategy, and introduces key ideas and tools to use in developing an organisational strategy.

Chapter 3 covers organisational leadership – How can managers balance the different roles that they are expected to play? It looks at different styles of leadership and the skills needed to manage a developing organisation.

The fourth chapter looks at the development of different types of organisational structures and suggests ways of managing structures and making changes to how your organisation is organised.

Chapter 5 is on the theme of working together. Organisations are having to find ways of cooperating and working together and this section suggests different ways in which such cooperation can be structured and methods of bringing it about.

Chapter 6 covers projects and teams. Increasingly organisations are creating short-term projects and teams to carry out specific tasks. This section looks at how internal projects can be established, designed and managed. It also outlines ways of encouraging team work.

The concluding chapter looks at managing organisational change. It suggests different approaches to change, introduces some practical tools that managers can use and deals with common problems in changing organisations.

There is also a final section offering some further reading and a brief guide to using external management consultants to help with organisational development.

Whilst the book need not be read from cover to cover, it is recommended that the introductory chapters be read first. Chapters 3–6, covering different issues, can be read in any order, finishing with chapter 7.

Case studies, diagrams and exercises punctuate the main text, giving you practical examples and helping you apply general advice to your individual organisation.

DEVELOPING YOUR ORGANISATION

We expect a lot from our organisations. They need to be flexible enough to cope with change and also secure enough to provide an efficient and stable place for people to work in. They need to be open to new ideas and able to welcome in new people and at the same time foster a sense of belonging. They need to be efficient – run in such a way that external agencies such as funders feel confident about investing in them. Yet organisations also need to encourage creativity and be responsive to change. Although we expect a lot from them we give little thought to their design, development and fitness for the task facing them.

> If our organisation was a motor vehicle it would have failed its MOT and been off the road years ago. Many of the controls no longer work. It's held together by odd bits of string and sticking plaster. The engine is badly out of condition. It rarely starts on time.
> *Anon – manager in a not for profit agency.*

Often our organisations and workplaces frustrate us. Good work, when it happens, seems to happen despite the organisation and those that manage it. Out of date systems, top-heavy structures and practices conspire to block progress. Many of our organisations and ways of working are inadequate and demoralising. Often organisations are slow to adapt to meet new circumstances and challenges.

There has been a rapid growth of interest in management and organisations. Numerous management books and training courses offer insight into the latest idea that will transform your organisation. So called management gurus and consultants have earned a fortune from selling their recipe for how to improve or change organisations. However, many of these ideas have fallen away and been dismissed as fads or temporary solutions. This book gives practical advice on organisational development without unnecessary jargon.

What makes up an organisation?

Organisations are composed of lots of different elements. Some are very obvious and tangible whilst others are harder to describe and deal with:

Purpose

All organisations were created for a purpose and in the absence of making money, not for profit agencies need a clear purpose to give them a rationale and meaning. Over time, the purpose often gets lost or becomes confused. Keeping going and survival is not enough.

Strategy and direction

It is not enough to know why you exist and what it is you want to do. You also need a strategy to get you there. Strategy can involve difficult decisions such as which activities to focus on and which ones to drop.

Power

Power exists in all organisations. Some of it is obvious, where the select few can make decisions and act independently whilst others have to seek permission before acting. Power can be concentrated in the hands of one or two people or it can be shared around the organisation. However, identifying power in an organisation is not straightforward. An organisational structure chart might show one view of who is in charge, but reality might be different. For example a group of staff and volunteers might have considerable power to stop something by refusing to cooperate. It is worth making the effort to understand the formal and informal power structures that operate in an organisation.

Management

Management is all about making things happen. It is about organising, planning, controlling and sometimes about leading. How our organisations are managed varies a lot depending on the skills, style and attitude of those responsible for managing.

Structures

How an organisation operates is determined by how it is structured. There are many different ways of structuring work: by geography (northern division/eastern office), by type of work (advice service/training unit/admin. department), by user (work with young people). Structures provide boundaries and a framework for communication and management.

Systems/processes

To make the organisation work, systems and processes are needed to ensure that decisions and information flow, that work happens, that resources are properly used and that the organisation and people in it are accountable. With too many systems and processes the organisation becomes bureaucratic: more time is spent servicing the system than doing work that meets the organisation's purpose. Without systems and processes everything depends on the style and preferences of the individuals involved.

Culture

Culture is hard to define and hard to measure exactly. It is the shared set of behaviours, styles and attitudes that influence how the organisation works (or does not work). In some places the culture is very strong and influences every aspect of the organisation. In others the culture might be changing, less clear or there may be several different cultures operating.

People

Organisations also have to cope with the peculiar set of personalities, egos and individual idiosyncrasies that make up people at work. Organisations need to be designed and developed in a way that brings out the best in people, encourages creativity and flexibility and makes for a productive workplace.

About organisational development

All organisations at some stage have problems. Some can be managed, but others become serious, create tensions and conflicts and can produce major dysfunction. Often managers fail to act and simply let the problem get worse. Organisational development is a series of processes and activities that aim to strengthen an organisation and make it fit for its purpose. Organisational development should have the following features:

1 Future focused

Organisational development should help the organisation understand and respond to changes in the outside world. It should help it to anticipate and respond to change and help the people responsible for the organisation's leadership think about how the organisation might grow, develop and change.

2 Direction setting

An organisational development process should help the organisation to be more strategic, focus on its priorities, make useful plans and agree how its human, financial and other resources can best be used to meet its priorities.

3

3 Unblocking the organisation

Organisational development is an opportunity to check on the effectiveness of the structures, systems and processes that the organisation uses. It should help the organisation to renew and improve its internal organisation and overcome practices that block effective and productive working.

4 Whole system based

An organisational development approach should recognise that change in one aspect of the organisation will usually create spin-off changes in other areas of the organisation. A new organisational strategy will have impact on the structures, systems and working practices of the organisation. The whole system needs to be considered – not just one aspect of it.

Organisational development is about helping an organisation to strengthen itself, be clear about its future role and strategy and build processes and structures that work. It is more a process or a journey than a single task.

A hierarchy of issues

In organisational development it is useful to work through a hierarchy of issues: Purpose – Strategy – Organisation – People

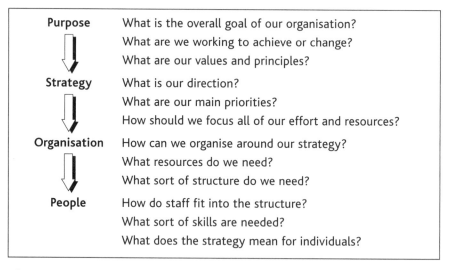

Purpose	What is the overall goal of our organisation?
	What are we working to achieve or change?
	What are our values and principles?
Strategy	What is our direction?
	What are our main priorities?
	How should we focus all of our effort and resources?
Organisation	How can we organise around our strategy?
	What resources do we need?
	What sort of structure do we need?
People	How do staff fit into the structure?
	What sort of skills are needed?
	What does the strategy mean for individuals?

The organisation's *purpose* is why it exists and is often called its mission statement. The purpose of the organisation represents its vision and values. It is best expressed in terms of the benefits or gains it seeks for the people who either use it or are intended to benefit from it.

The *strategy* is the direction that the organisation will follow to meet its purpose. The strategy sets out the priorities where the organisation will use its resources and efforts.

The *organisation* is the collection of structures, systems, boundaries and roles that will be used to do the work and control and supervise people's roles and contributions.

The *people* are the members of the organisation who manage the organisation, support its activities and do the work.

It is important to try to be systematic in working through the four levels. They connect together and need to follow on from each other. If they do not, problems and mismatches can occur:

Strategy without purpose

Decisions about strategy often appear as an organisation arrives at a crossroads. Examples might be: should we take on a new service or should we withdraw from an area of work? The solution or preferred strategy must be tested against a clear statement of purpose. Everything that the organisation does should fit with the purpose. It is all too easy to undertake activities and follow strategies that do not tie in with the purpose – examples include doing something because some funding became available or running an activity or project because a member of staff likes it and enjoys it.

Organisation without strategy

Only review or change your organisation when you are clear on what sort of strategy or direction you intend to follow. Organisation should flow from strategy. Decisions about how to organise work, what sort of structure to use and how job roles should develop all need to be informed by the organisation's strategic direction. If an organisation is designed or restructured without a clear sense of strategy there is a danger that the organisation will not be fit for its purpose.

People factors dominate

Often organisational change is blocked by resistance or inertia from people in the organisation. They are reluctant to develop or learn new skills to move into new roles. They prefer to work in established ways or structures. In organisational development and strategy work it is important to look first at how the organisation can best meet its users' needs and then determine strategies and structures to do so. Developing a strategy or way of working around the interests of the people who work in the organisation may avoid conflict or difficult decisions, but will in the medium- to longer-term damage the effectiveness and value of the organisation.

Getting started on organisational development
Strategy before structure

Often organisations spend considerable time and effort reorganising without a real idea of how they want the organisation to develop or what direction they want it to follow. A trustee of a voluntary organisation described how in her organisation 'we are in a constant state of reorganisation – new structures, new job descriptions and so on. We have never sat down and worked out what we want the organisation to do and then decided how best to organise to get there'. Form should follow function. The structure (job roles, organisational boundaries and reporting lines) should be organised in such a way that helps the organisation follow its strategy rather than block it.

The process is key

In organisational development, the way in which the process is managed is critical to its success. Staff, board members, volunteers and others with a stake in the organisation need to feel that they have been involved in the process, have actively contributed to it and have been listened to. If the process is an effective one then people are more likely to understand and take on board changes involved. Designing and managing the process is hard and if discussions and decisions are rushed people may feel uninvolved and lack commitment to the outcome. On the other hand, an ineffective process can lead to long drawn out consultation meetings, discussions that either go nowhere or produce results that are, in order to avoid conflict, so insubstantial and weak that they fail to make any real difference.

Manage change

Bringing about change at work can be an arduous and thankless task. Often change produces conflict, anxiety and disruption. Sometimes resistance can be surprising. One worker in an international development agency described her reaction to a plan for change in her organisation. 'I could see the rationale behind the plan and recognise that many aspects of the current organisation set-up do not work at all well. However at least I understand the current set-up and know how to operate in it'. Managers need to think about and develop strategies, processes and approaches that support and enable change.

Don't copy ... think

Real organisational development cannot simply be copied from elsewhere. To develop an organisation you need to understand the context, history and issues that make it up. You also need to develop a process that brings together all of the different interests in the organisation who have a stake in its future.

20 point health check

This quick exercise is a simple way of taking stock of how your organisation operates. It is useful to get a few people to do the exercise individually and then compare notes. Once the results have been gathered the following three points are useful to focus discussion.

■ Are there any common themes in your answers?

■ Which questions need attention?
  (give examples of things that work or do not work to illustrate)

■ Which aspects of the organisation work well?
  (Why? What do we need to do to keep it working well?)

It is a rough and ready exercise. You need to respect the fact that each individual has their own perception of what is good or is not good. The organisation is changing all the time. What is important is the discussion it opens up amongst colleagues, as that should help to focus on how best to develop your organisation.

Scoring

Look at each statement and score them on the following basis:

0 – strongly disagree   1 – disagree   2 – agree   3 – strongly agree

1   There is usually cooperation between different parts of the organisation ☐

2   The management board/committee makes time to look at the strategic issues facing the organisation ☐

3   Our overall purpose and vision is clear ☐

4   We keep up to date with developments and trends in our sector ☐

5   We are able to demonstrate the results of our work ☐

6   Communication within the organisation is good. The left hand usually knows what the right hand is doing ☐

7   Everyone is involved in the process of agreeing future strategy and making plans ☐

8   Managers have time to evaluate, plan and develop the organisation ☐

9   We regularly review the effectiveness of our work ☐

10 Responsibilities for decision making are clear ☐

11 There are structures and systems to ensure accountability and reporting back throughout the organisation ☐

12 The culture at work encourages fresh thinking and change ☐

13 We have a clear sense of direction for the next few years ☐

14 There is a good flow of information that helps review progress and make decisions ☐

15 We put time and resources into developing new ideas and projects ☐

16 The way that we are structured is effective and flexible ☐

17 The management committee regularly reviews progress and achievements against plans ☐

18 There is a strong sense of commitment to a shared set of values and ethos ☐

19 There is a strong sense of teamwork ☐

20 We regularly put time aside to develop and improve our work ☐

Place your score next to the corresponding question number and then add up each line to reach your total score for each factor:

Factor					total score
Learning and development	5 ___	9 ___	15 ___	20 ___	___
Internal Process	6 ___	10 ___	14 ___	16 ___	___
Strategy	3 ___	4 ___	7 ___	13 ___	___
Governance and management	2 ___	8 ___	11 ___	17 ___	___
Style and culture	1 ___	12 ___	18 ___	19 ___	___

Learning and development is about the internal capacity in the organisation to evaluate and learn from what you do and ensure that the organisation is being effective.

Internal process is about how the organisation works and operates. It relates to internal systems and mechanisms for communication and coordination.

Strategy is about the organisation's clarity of direction, focus and priority.

Governance and management relates to the processes for managing the organisation and in particular the roles of the Board (trustees or committee) and paid management staff.

Style and culture is about the atmosphere, working and management style and traditions that dominate how the organisation works.

A quick guide to management speak

In the past few years telling people how to manage or change their organisation has become a boom industry. New ideas, strategies and jargon are constantly being launched. Many of them have sound and useful things in them. Others are simply passing fashions. Here are sixteen of the most common. Don't try them all at once!

Change agent – Someone responsible for introducing and managing an organisational change.

Customer focused – Taking the user/client seriously – listening to their views and designing services around their needs and wants as opposed to designing things for the convenience of the organisation.

Downsizing and delayering – Cutting the number of middle management jobs. Reducing the number of levels in the hierarchy to create an organisation that communicates faster, moves quicker and is customer focused.

Empowerment – Letting staff make decisions and take greater responsibility.

Intellectual capital – The value of the organisation is not just the tangible assets. It is also the individual and collective knowledge, competence and 'know how'. Such knowledge needs protecting, valuing and reinforcing.

Knowledge management – The process of working out what expertise and knowledge there is in the organisation and deciding how to share it and use it.

Learning organisation – A philosophy that encourages active learning by all members of the organisation. Through this process it is able to grow, develop and transform itself.

Outsourcing – Rather than run and manage an activity or service yourself, contract with someone else to do it for you.

Performance management – A management system based on defining expectations, delegation coaching, feedback and appraisal.

Risk management – Auditing what could go wrong, making people aware of risks and having preventative measures in place.

Self directed teams – Setting up project teams and task groups that are so clear about their task that they are able to manage and direct themselves with only minimal input from formal managers.

Stakeholder management – A recognition that lots of different people and groups have an interest in the organisation, and managing in such a way to keep stakeholders on board and committed to your plans.

Total quality management – A framework of processes and systems to create and improve the quality elements of how a service is managed, organised and delivered.

Transparency – Having a management and organisational culture that is open and in which decisions and information are discussed openly rather than in secret.

Virtual organisation – A network of organisations, groups and people coming together to do a particular task without a formal organisational or business structure.

360 degree feedback – A process by which individuals or organisations can gather feedback from all the key stakeholders who have contact with them.

STRATEGY

Strategy and strategic planning are accepted in most organisations as being needed. It is as if managers feel naked if they have not got an impressive and inspiring strategic plan to show off to the outside world. Valuable time and money is spent on away days, consultants and other attempts to agree and document a strategy. But many managers suffer from SPOTS – Strategic Plans on Top Shelf. The plan once agreed and written up is filed away never to be looked at again.

The manager of a community enterprise agency described her experience in the following way: 'We spent ages producing a strategic plan. We started out with bold and imaginative ideas. They soon got lost in long and confused discussions. We got stuck over exactly what was our "mission" and got confused about the difference between aims, objectives, goals and visions. In the end we produced a written document that says very little and no one takes any notice of.'

This chapter aims to do three things:

- To define strategy in a way that is useful to an organisation and is more than just another empty and time consuming management game.
- To introduce a framework and process for building and agreeing a strategy for your organisation.
- To look at how the process of agreeing a future strategy can bring together different people and interests in the organisation and hopefully create a shared commitment to its implementation.

What is strategy?

Many definitions of strategy imply an exact and perfect plan. Many examples of strategy come from the military: the art of manoeuvring an army to win a battle. Commercial companies often borrow this language and talk of strategies to 'beat the opposition' or win a 'competitive battle'. However, strategy for not for profit agencies is a different activity. Effective and sound strategy should have the following elements:

- It helps the organisation to focus on or renew its purpose and vision.
- It enables the organisation to develop priorities and plans that enable it to respond to changes, opportunities and threats in the outside world.

- It should build commitment amongst key people in the organisation to the organisation's future direction and priorities.

Many managers find working on strategic issues hard and off-putting. The idea of spending time planning a future strategy does not appeal. The organisation is too busy doing its work to plan; too many things are changing too fast to plan; many elements, such as future funding, are unknown and discussions about direction and future priorities can always be put off until another day. The process of putting the plan together can seem like hard work and is often neglected. However, not planning or not even thinking about future strategy can cause serious harm to the health of an organisation. The following four problems can occur:

1   **The organisation gets bounced from issue to issue**
    The organisation fails to anticipate changes in the world outside. It only changes when it has to. It is reactive and often in a state of crisis.

2   **The organisation has to follow other people's agenda**
    The organisation is led by other people's decisions. Funders or other similar organisations set the pace and the direction. The organisation either copies what others are doing or feels obliged to follow their strategy.

3   **The organisation gets stuck**
    In the absence of any clear direction the organisation simply falls back on what it has always done in the past. The organisation's pattern of services and activities, its budget and the way it uses its resources are driven by history rather than any fresh thinking.

4   **There is confusion and possibly conflict in the organisation**
    Often people in the organisation have different views on what it is for, what is the organisation's ethos and what are the main priorities. The organisation is continually being pulled in several different directions at once.

It is possible to live with these four factors and manage around them. However, often a point is reached where management must act and start the process of clarifying purpose, direction and priorities.

The language of strategy

To help understand the role of strategy in the context of an organisation it is useful to think of our organisations as having three different levels of managing:

The **big picture** – This level is about the organisation's reason for existing: its overall rationale and purpose. Questions at this level are about long-term concepts, visions and policy:

Why do we do exist?
What is our vision?
What values do we hold?
What are we for?

Vision: What we are for – our purpose

Values: What we stand for – our ethos

The **strategic** level – This level is about how to implement the mission and goals set out in the big picture level. It is about turning ideas and aspirations into action and reality.

What is the direction?
What are our priorities for the next few years?
Where should we put most of our effort?
What needs to change?

The **activity** level – This level is about the day-to-day work of the organisation. It is the most tangible and easy to measure level.

What gets done on a week to week basis?
How do we ensure that activities and services are delivered?
How de we allocate resources, time and energy?
How do we manage and organise properly?

Often these three levels do not work or fit together at all well. In some organisations senior managers or headquarters policy units produce new policies without much thought of what kind of strategy is needed to implement them or the operational realities and problems facing people delivering services.

Often policy makers become frustrated that people at an activity level do not see the need for new policies. People at the activity level just wish that they could be left alone to get on with their work.

There can be a lack of any feedback and communication between the three levels. There is no encouragement or process for people doing the day-to-day work to contribute to strategy or policy making.

The strategy level should link together the organisation's aspirations and its day-to-day work. For these three levels to work the strategic level must have three parts to it:

1   **Priorities**
    The strategic level must make clear what is and what is not a priority. It is easy to avoid being clear about priorities and pretending that everything is important. Often it takes an element of management courage to say

that something might be needed, important and relevant, but can not be a priority. How the organisation uses its resources should be reviewed to ensure that they reflect the priorities.

2 **Communication**
The strategic level brings together the different levels. It should help staff see their work in a bigger context and explain why the organisation does things. It should also feed back useful information about what is really happening in the organisation to people involved in making policy.

3 **Change**
Strategic management is very much about change management. A new or updated strategy usually requires some kind of change. Some activities and services expand and grow, others might close or decline. Staff may have to develop new skills and play new roles. Existing structures and systems need to be modernised or changed to meet the new strategy. All of these changes need careful and skilful management.

Common blocks to strategic management

The following three problems can make strategic management and work on strategy difficult:

1 **The organisation tries to be all things to all people – it fails to set, or keep to priorities**
The organisation is unclear as to what is its current purpose and intention. It covers too many issues. Services, projects and activities do not connect together into a coherent picture. Everything is seen as being important and urgent. The organisation dabbles in many different issues or drifts from idea to idea.

2 **There is no organisational learning**
The emphasis is on being busy all of the time. There is not time to think, evaluate current activities or take stock of how the organisation is doing. There is very little organised learning from experience.

3 **The organisation is not specific about outcomes**
Outcomes are the benefits, results and changes made as a result of the organisation's activities and outputs. They represent the ends (e.g. 'a healthier lifestyle' or 'a reduction in street crime') as opposed to the means (e.g. 'a mobile health clinic open for 20 hours' or 'three projects lasting six months working with young offenders'). Often we spend so much time managing and organising the *means* that we lose sight of the *ends*. Good strategy has to come from a clear sense of *why* we are doing something and what we want to achieve.

Getting the process right

The way you go about strategic planning has significant impact on the usefulness of the exercise. If key people (staff, supporters, board members etc) are involved in discussion about strategy and are actively involved in making plans, then there is a good chance that they will support or at the very least understand the changes involved. Managing the process is key. People need to know how they will be involved, what sort of consultation is possible, and the process and timescale for making decisions.

At the start it is useful to stress that in the process everything is up for grabs. Organisational goals, roles, structures and purpose can all be evaluated, questioned and challenged. The strategic process is a rare chance to have a structured and creative think about what the organisation is for, what its direction should be and what should be its future goals.

For it to work it needs a willingness to learn and a commitment to see the process through. As part of the development, people must be willing to question why the organisation does things and how effective it is. The status quo or the way things have always been done may be challenged. This can be an exciting and lively time, but it can make some people defensive, anxious and apprehensive. The process needs to be managed in such a way that on one level people feel safe in the discussion, are encouraged to express their view and participate but on another level, difficult issues are not avoided and challenges are not fudged.

The people leading the process may well need skills in managing change, participation and possibly conflict.

A simple strategic framework

The following framework maps out a process that an organisation could use to develop or update its strategy. Every organisation is different and therefore the framework needs adapting to take into account the organisation's size, style and structure.

1 First base

The first stage involves asking simple questions to check that the organisation has a clear and relevant sense of purpose. In the management jargon of our times this is called producing a mission statement. Often people can be cynical about mission statement. They think that managers spend too much time playing around with innocuous buzz words trying to produce a snappy statement; that its only real purpose is to be hung up in the reception area.

Despite this cynicism, it is important to check at the start of the exercise that there is a clear and united view of what is the purpose of the organisation and what set of values or ethos holds it together and influences all of its work.

The following questions are good starting points:

What are we for?

If we did not exist why would we need to be invented? What 'ends' are we trying to create? What do we want to change or make different? These question should tease out some sense of what is the vision behind the organisation's work. Usually when an organisation is first established the vision is the driving force. It creates a focus for people's energy and enthusiasm. Over times things change, new needs and new philosophies emerge. It is therefore important to check that a common thread links all the activities together.

Losing the plot

It is easy for the organisation's activities, services and funding to take up so much time and energy that the reason for doing things becomes confused, obscure or even ignored. Here are three examples:

Who is it for?

The staff and manager of a charity's family centre could not agree on the seemingly simple question of who the centre was for. Was the centre there to look after the needs of children, their parents or the whole family? Or was it there to meet the needs of the local authority social services department who referred families to the centre and paid for the centre's work? As one worker put it, 'Lots of disagreements in the centre about policy, standards and future plans could be traced back to this issue. We cannot agree on whose interest we are working in and how we balance the interests of other stakeholders'.

What are we meant to be?

Downtown People's Centre has always prided itself on being 'run by and for' the local people who live in the area. Two years ago the management committee agreed to the centre becoming part of a consortia of community groups to bid for and deliver vocational training courses funded by the European Union. The centre's two staff had to stop doing their community development and neighbourhood support work to ensure that the centre could recruit the fifteen students. Much of their time has gone on supporting the courses, helping the students and dealing with the complex administration involved. The long standing chair of the management committee has just announced her intention to stand down: 'All of our resources and time have gone into the training programme. Yes, it is important, but it has taken us away from serving the needs of all the local people – we have drifted into being a mini college and part of the education and training system'.

Campaigner or partner?

GreenCo had a long track record as a successful environmental conservation project. It had developed several recycling and conservation schemes alongside its campaigning and educational work. A new director described the strategic problems confronting her: 'Part of the organisation sees its role in a very business-like way – taking on consultancies to improve environmental practices and winning local authority contracts for recycling initiatives. Another part of the organisation wants us to do more campaigning work and expose the poor and bad practices of some of the local authorities. We have contracts with these authorities. We have to decide if we are a campaigning organisation or a service provider. Can we really be both? We have grown so fast that it is hard to work out what we are supposed to be'.

What is different about us?

A useful way to probe this issue is to identify what is different about the organisation compared to other similar agencies. In marketing terms this is known as your USP; your unique selling proposition. One training agency recognised that there were many other organisations running courses for unemployed people. They identified their key difference was that they took a more holistic approach to their students. Not only did they provide training courses, but unlike other agencies they provided one-to-one support, learning skills support, child care, careers advice and other support services. These additional services gave the agency the edge over others.

What is important to us?

Often what distinguishes an organisation or makes it different is not what it does, but its style and the practical application of its ethos and philosophy. These factors, often called values, are the organising principles that should influence all aspects of how the organisation functions and how it works with other people. A newly appointed Director of a housing project described the importance of values in her organisation: 'I made it a priority to get people talking about what they saw our core values as being. We needed a consistent and simple values statement so that staff would know how we should treat users and also how the organisation and colleagues should treat them. The work on values was all about changing our culture from one in which we as professionals always knew best to one in which we offered choices, rights and responsibilities to our users.'

This stage is about asking fundamental questions that help to define the organisation. In some organisations answering them is a fairly straightforward and unchallenging task. The stage can be done quite quickly. In others the questions raise profound and difficult issues that sometimes question the very reasons why the organisation does what it does and even why it should continue to exist. Common problems or conflicts include:

Tangible means and invisible ends

People understand and can see the work and activity of the organisation. They can measure, judge and manage the means. All discussions are about how to manage the means – do more of … organise better … expand or contract. They are unable or unwilling to talk about why things are done or the longer-term purpose. The means overshadow the ends.

Founder's vision versus today's reality

Any statement of mission or organisational aims and objectives can become out of date. New ideas, new realities and social change can make the original founding statement or legal objectives feel dated. One children's charity realised that the vision of original founders was that the organisation would work with 'waifs and strays' and manage large institutions and orphanages. The charity had moved on from that kind of work years ago. It needed to create a new modern vision for the organisation that reflected today's needs and values.

Being funder driven

It is easy to be led or strongly influenced by funding policies and the interests of funders. One manager commented that in reality the overriding vision of his organisation had been to 'do whatever brought in money'. He described how the organisation would regularly reinvent itself to fit in with whatever was on the funder's agenda: 'Over the past four years we have been a counselling centre, a health project, a drop in centre, an outreach project, an advice agency, a training centre and a community resource centre. We keep dreaming up schemes to fit with whatever funders are into. As a consequence we have lost any coherent sense of identity and direction. We have got to find a focus for the organisation that is more than year to year survival.'

2 Learning

Before being able to develop a strategy there is a need to take stock of the organisation's development to date and also to spot how changes in its external environment could affect it. This phase is about organisational learning and evaluation. It involves gathering hard and soft information to help strategic thinking. Hard information is fact based and is about such questions as: How many people use this service? What is the unit cost? What is the level of demand? Hard information should be objective and dispassionate. Soft information is about people's feelings, opinions and perceptions. Such questions ask: What do users, funders and staff think about our services? What do people like or dislike? How do we compare to other agencies? Soft information is harder to quantify and be exact about. It comes more from conversations than from surveys or quantifiable methods. Getting the balance right is important. Strategic planning needs to be based on data and also on people's opinions and judgments.

Two issues can help to inform strategic discussions:

A review of what works

What is the organisation good at? What aspects of our work produce results and outcomes? Often we fail to recognise, share and celebrate achievements and successes. One simple idea is to organise future strategy around what you do well – your key talents. For example, one social care organisation realised that it had particular skills and expertise in supporting young people leaving care. It decided to specialise in this work and build upon its successful track record.

A scan of how the external environment is changing

Good strategy comes from understanding the world in which you operate and being able to anticipate and respond to changes. Often we fail to do this. We become so focused on the internal life of the organisation that we fail to see trends and changes in the world outside.

One creative technique for doing this scan is based on an established strategic planning process called scenario planning. This involves:

Fast forwarding

Start by planning where you want to get to in three or five years and then work back to where you are now. You need to be willing to stand back from how the organisation is now and think about how it could be in the future. The problems, structures and circumstances of how you are now should not constrain your creativity.

Future search

This involves identifying trends, opportunities, changes and factors in the outside world that could have impact on how you operate. Possible trends include:

Changes in needs and expectations

What changes might take place in your user or client base or profile? This could include hard factors such as demographic changes (e.g. more people living longer) or softer factors such as changes in expectation (e.g. clients having higher or more diverse expectations of you).

Changes in technology and in how we organise work

This section might include changes in how the organisation works and the way work is carried out. Examples might include: new professional practices or standards; changes in working practices (e.g. more outreach work – less centre-based work); and changes in technology (e.g. more people having access to communications technology).

Changes in how we live and work

Social change can have a major impact on your work. Examples of trends might include changes in family make-up, changes in working patterns and other cultural changes.

Political and economic changes

This could include new legislation, new government direction or policy (e.g. on social exclusion) or changes in the economic arena.

External trends

The Bleakside Development Agency (BDA) was set up to help cope with the impact of large scale factory closures and increased long-term unemployment. The agency provided an advice service, a base for community activities and ran various campaigns and initiatives to ensure that 'local people played a full part in the regeneration of the Bleakside area'.

The agency decided to take a day to develop a future strategy and followed the process described in this chapter of identifying future trends and their implications.

Staff, committee members and volunteers spent time brainstorming future trends and issues that could affect their work. After twenty minutes nearly thirty different issues were listed. Some of the issues listed were based on known fact, other were based on judgments or on practical experience.

It was agreed that the top ten key issues for BDA were:

1   Growing local inequality

2   Increased debt problems – more loan sharks operating locally

3   More older people needing support

4   Need for BDA to be businesslike – funders want performance measures, business plans, targets

5   The Government's social exclusion agenda

6   EU funding could decline

7   Funders want innovation – project rather than core funding

8   Younger people involved in drug misuse

9   Some institutions, e.g. local banks and shops, moving off the estate

10   Some new business start ups – local skills shortages

The list led to a very thorough debate about how the agency could respond. After some discussion everyone agreed that BDA had to respond to these changes. It could not choose to stay as it was.

The group then spent time looking at how BDA could respond. Several possible scenarios were designed. One was that BDA should focus on money advice, help people with long-term debts and encourage the setting up of a local credit union. Another was that BDA should move into vocational training and bid to run courses for long-term unemployed people.

After this discussion twelve options and choices were prepared for a full meeting. Options and choices included:

Should the centre become a base for vocational training?
Should we be about economic development rather than only community development?
Should we develop a home visiting advice service for elderly people?
Should we investigate the feasibility of community businesses (e.g. a food co-op) to replace businesses leaving the estate?

The management committee narrowed the list of twelve options down to a list of three high priority issues, three medium ones, four low priority issues and two issues not to proceed on. This provided the basis for BDA's business plan and also several successful project funding bids.

One worker commented that the process did three things: 'It helped people to see the bigger picture. Identifying trends and external issues was hard work at first, but it really helped to create an agenda for change. Secondly, it stopped complacency. It was obvious that we could not stay as we were. We had to respond and change. Finally, identifying options and choices for the agency felt very positive. It meant that we could be outward looking and take the initiative, rather than sit waiting for something to happen.'

How other organisations might develop

This area is focused on the direction taken by organisations that might do similar work to yours. Their strategy could have a direct or indirect effect on your work.

Changes in the resources available for your work

This section is an attempt to identify changes in the resources available for your work. It should take into account non-financial as well as financial resources – volunteers, staff skills and other things that the organisation needs. Issues here could include: How do we see our fundraising income developing? What might be the balance between grant aid, contract work and public fundraising?

The list of issues produced will consist of some items that are definite and exact. Others may be based on a trend or a feeling, some more on guesswork. The more people who contribute to the list, the more extensive and richer it becomes. Once a full list has been produced it is worth looking at the following four questions:

> Which of the issues listed are critical ones for us?
> What potential opportunities are there for us?
> What potential threats are there for us?
> What sort of strategic options are available to positively respond to this environment?

One useful and often creative technique is to ask people to design or draw (often people find it easier to draw than to describe) two or three possible scenarios of how the organisation might be if the identified trends happen. Different kinds of scenarios are possible:

Radical scenarios: The organisation would be significantly different. It would do things differently from how it operates now. This would represent a major change or even relaunch.

Adaptive or gradual scenarios: The organisation would try to stay the same, but adapt and respond to the trends identified. The organisation would try to incorporate changes.

Bleak scenarios: What would happen if the trends were mainly threats or the organisation failed to respond effectively? In the light of all the changes can the organisation stay as it is?

3 Options and choices

This stage is about making decisions and developing a strategy that is clear and gives a focused direction to the organisation. It builds on the previous stage. Participants need to be informed by and learn from the discussions and work carried out.

The scenarios outlined in the previous stage should open up debate and discussions about what options might be available. Issues for debate could include:

Should we do more of x and less of y?

Do we grow, stay the same or contract?

How might our current services and activities need to change?

What should be our top priorities?

Where do we want to be in three years' time?

Three things are important in this discussion. First, that all participants have had the chance to consider and learn about the key changes taking place or likely to take place in the organisation's environment. Secondly, that the discussion is not weighed down by the constraints and circumstances of how the organisation is now. Issues of funding, staffing and current expectations are important, but are secondary to direction. Decide where you want to go first and then look at the organisational and resource implications of how to get there. Thirdly, watch out for difficult decisions and choices being avoided or fudged. Often management committees or staff groups will operate as if everything is important so everything must be a priority. This simply stores up problems for later. A good process should allow for full discussion, consultation and participation, but it cannot avoid the fact that sometimes difficult and unpopular choices have to be made.

Management by avoidance

Fran was a new and committed member of the Board of the Heathcliff Arts Development Agency. The agency employed four staff who used different art forms in various community development and education projects.

At the second meeting that Fran attended the board decided to have an away day to agree a future strategy for the agency. The agency had a good external reputation, but there was a feeling that it was losing its way and lacked any coherent direction.

So, a few weeks later all of the staff and most of the board met to spend a day looking at future strategy. Most of the morning was spent reviewing the development and work of the agency so far. As Fran listened to what was being said she started to feel that people were avoiding two issues:

It seemed as if Dave, one of the workers, wanted the agency to work only with young people. All of his contributions were about the importance of arts work with young people. Whenever he spoke the other staff did not say anything, but looked frustrated.

A year ago the agency had won a contract to develop a cybercafé to encourage interest in information technology. It seemed as if the project had been disappointing. Take up had been slow. There had been several delays in getting it up and running. Costs and staff time involved in running it were much greater than originally estimated. It still had two more years' funding, but Fran had picked up that the funding body was concerned about it.

Fran felt that whenever these two issues were raised they were dodged. Over lunch she suggested to the Chair of the Agency's Board that it would be useful to spend time deciding who were the agency's main priority users and also discuss what to do with the cybercafé project. The chair listened to Fran, but advised caution. She did not want to 'rock the boat' or raise conflicts. Reluctantly, Fran did not raise the issues.

After the away day a 'strategic plan' was produced that was very positive about the agency. It described it as 'promoting art for all the community' and gave no real direction or answers to the issues Fran had identified.

Three months later the management board's meeting was dominated by a feeling of internal crisis. The staff team were at loggerheads. Conflicts had arisen over Dave's insistence that only work with young people was of any value. The team felt weighed down by conflicts. The cybercafé was in trouble and its funders had written to express their concern at poor performance. It seemed that the agency had lost interest in it. The Board could only come up with lots of remedial or short-term action plans.

Fran could not help wondering if this was all a consequence of avoiding issues in the strategic planning day. Why had these issues not been identified, discussed openly and resolved?

Discussion:

Are there any examples of management avoidance in your organisation?
What hidden agendas need to be brought to the surface?
How can you manage the process?

The strategy, once agreed on, should be expressed in terms that are clear, unambiguous and transparent. It should be communicated in such a way that people working in or connected to the organisation can see the relevance to them and identify the implications.

4 Putting it together

The next and final stage involves turning the strategy into practical action. Often this stage involves the production of a business plan that sets out a statement of intent, outlines the assumptions that have been made about future trends, makes a measurable plan and makes clear the resource needs of the organisation. The following issues need consideration here:

How will we resource the plan?

Often the strategy only becomes real for people when money, resources and time are allocated to it. Is the strategy totally dependent on 'new' money and other resources being found or will existing resources be diverted to it? How might changes in the level of resources (e.g. a downturn in fundraising) affect the strategy?

What are the details of implementation?

The strategy sets out a clear direction. The next stage is to turn it into something that is a guide to action. The language changes as strategy is developed. The language of mission statements is one of aspiration and will (e.g. 'to create a strong and sustainable local economy'). Strategic language is focused and more committed (e.g. 'to develop services that support the creation of community businesses and enterprises'). You need to develop action plans or SMART objectives – Specific Measurable Agreed Resourced and Timed (e.g. by February to have successfully run three four-day training programmes for potential community business managers). The action plan needs to be tight. It should assign responsibility and resources and make measurement possible.

What changes need to be managed?

It is worthwhile to identify changes that are likely to be needed as a result of the strategy. Some may be obvious – the strategic decision to move into a new area of work will require new skills, new knowledge and possibly new ways of managing. Some changes may be less obvious – the change in the organisation's style or culture might be harder to describe or be exact about, but could be critical to the success of a new strategy. Time spent anticipating changes needed and identifying what can be done to help people change usually helps managers to prevent disruption and uncertainty that may obstruct or delay the implementation of a new strategy.

The budget as a block to strategy

In many organisations, large or small, the task of putting the budget together is often an annual administrative or managerial chore delegated or dumped on the treasurer or finance department. Those tasked with the job use the most recent budget as their starting point. Expenditure on existing commitments in the shape of programmes and projects is calculated and income is then set against it. This process means that the budget is based on history rather than on future plans. A member of staff in one organisation described it in this way:

> 'Once something is in the budget it is inclined to reappear every year. On the other hand if you have a new idea it is usually likely to be rejected on the basis that "there is no money in the budget". That really is not true. There is money, but it is being spent on things we got into years ago.'

The budget is an important part of formulating strategy. Here are four ways to avoid the budget being a block to new strategies.

Time the process: Ensure that the process of agreeing an organisation-wide strategy and priorities happens before the budget process. The new strategy should identify priorities for budget change.

Identify possible movement: Some expenditure commitments are difficult to move or withdraw from. Others might be more amenable to change or redeployment to newer priorities. Identify possible areas for flexibility or movement.

Link the budget to activity: Often budgets use headings that might make administrative convenience, e.g. all expenditure on staff is grouped together in the salary budget; all expenditure on communication is put into a communication budget. An alternative is to use a cost- or activity-based budget system where all expenditure (including management costs) is allocated to the organisation's key programme areas or priorities. This system gives managers much clearer information on what a project actually costs and helps to evaluate priorities against spending patterns.

Zero-based budgeting: One technique is to rebuild the budget as if you were starting afresh without the legacy of past commitments and spending. What would the budget look like if it was geared around current priorities rather than past spending?

STRATEGY IMPLEMENTATION SHEET

This implementation sheet is used by one agency to turn its strategic plan into action

AREA OF WORK/PROJECT

To increase our membership and create a network of local campaigning groups

SUCCESS CRITERIA

To increase from 23 to 40 local support groups in two years

That 70% of local groups can function and campaign without constant field support

Individual membership up by 15%

Local income up by 10%

TARGET OUTPUTS

15% increase in membership

Functioning local groups in 40 areas

WORK PLAN – KEY TASKS/EVENTS/ACTIVITIES

Create new post of local groups support officer – Bob to lead

Set up local groups training session – Teri to lead

Run national membership campaign – Bob to lead

Run national media campaign – Sue to lead

Week of action in March – Bob to lead

RESOURCES REQUIRED

New post of local groups support officer

Budget bid by January

Review day in July

MILESTONES

Action plan by February

Quarterly board review

How do we check on the strategy?

The strategy needs to be described in such a way that progress, setbacks and actions can be clearly identified and monitored. It is useful to produce a simple implementation sheet for a new strategy that lists key milestones and predicts progress. Such activities can help to ensure that the strategy is kept alive, that managers return to it and feel responsible for it and that progress and hard work involved in implementing it can be recognised and acknowledged.

How strategic are you?

This quick exercise is a simple way of encouraging committee members, staff and others to evaluate how the strategic process of the organisation is managed. People should do it individually and then compare results. Discussion of the results should highlight what action is needed.

	strongly disagree	disagree	agree	strongly agree
1 We have a clear strategic direction for the next few years				
2 We are good at spotting trends and opportunities in the world outside				
3 We regularly review the effectiveness of our work				
4 We have very clear priorities for this year				
5 Our core purpose and mission is relevant, clear and up to date				
6 A strong sense of shared values underpins all our work				
7 All of our services and activities fit together into a strategy				
8 We regularly review our written plans				
9 Our future planning is usually realistic				
10 Our financial budget represents our priorities				

Frequently asked questions about strategy

What is strategic planning?

In organisational terms it is about three things:

> It is an organised and managed process.
>
> It enables an organisation to review progress, identify internal and external changes that might have an impact on the organisation and agree how best to respond.
>
> It leads to a clear direction and priorities and identifies changes that will be needed.

How does strategic planning differ from business planning?

In some situations the two are practically the same thing. The business plan represents a written statement of what the strategy is, how the strategy will be implemented and how the organisation will be organised and funded in order to meet the strategy. Discussions and agreement of strategy (direction and priorities) need to come before detailed planning of budgets and other organisational and business matters. A good business plan 'sets out your organisation's stall'. It outlines the organisational background and history, explains how you see the future and what your priorities should be and then sets out key assumptions about how the plan will be funded and resourced. Agree your strategic direction and then write the business plan.

How can you plan if everything keeps changing?

A good strategic process should help the organisation to identify and anticipate changes in your environment, which should make responding to change less reactive. If we refuse to think about or plan future strategy, the danger is that the organisation fails to respond to change and is bounced around from issue to issue. Strategic management helps prepare the organisation for change and develops skills in managing change.

What is the process for doing it?

The process is important. It needs to involve people throughout the organisation in reviewing progress, anticipating change, considering future options, making priorities and agreeing a future direction and plan. The process should be one that engages the organisation and creates full debate and discussion. It must also be one that is carefully managed to ensure that firm decisions and plans are made and that consultation and discussions have a practical value.

How long does it take?

The process does take some time. Often people need help to understand the process and the idea of strategy. Some people need to learn about the organisation and understand the issues facing it. It is useful to plan the process and agree a timetable for the work involved that allows space for people to get involved, but ensures that the process does not disrupt the organisation's work or drag on.

Who should do it?

The senior people in the organisation (e.g. trustees, board members and senior management) must show their commitment to the strategic process. They must make time to be involved in it. It is important that someone or some people should be delegated with the responsibility of leading and managing the process. This could be a senior manager or a task group of different people in the organisation, or an external consultant could be hired to help the process. Whoever leads the process will need skills in facilitating discussions and be able to act as a 'change agent'.

Ten ways to keep your strategic planning alive

It is easy to ignore the strategic plan once it has been produced. Often it simply becomes another document to be filed away and forgotten about. Here are ten practical ideas to keep your strategic plan and your organisation's sense of strategy alive.

1 Identify key milestones

Milestones are achievements in the implementation and delivery of your strategy. Examples include:

Completion of a feasibility study into a new service
Funds raised for pilot project
100 training places filled

Milestones work best if they are described as an achievement or point in the plan that recognises that one phase of the strategy has been completed and you can now move onto another phase. Milestones acknowledge progress and help to keep the strategy visible. They also provide an early warning device: if you cannot reach the milestone does the plan need rethinking or are extra efforts and resources needed?

2 Rolling plan

Often planners try to plan too far into the future. They write detailed plans and budgets for years ahead. The plan is discredited.
How can you produce a detailed plan for, say, three or five years' time? One way to overcome this is to produce a rolling plan that is regularly updated as the plan moves forward. The three levels of the plan are treated differently:

Mission: the organisation's reason for existing – its core purpose and values. Unless there are major changes we can assume that the vision and values will remain relevant for the medium- to long-term – check them every 3/5 years.

Strategy: the organisation's main direction and priorities for the next few years. Review your strategy at least annually – check on its implementation and progress. Update and revise as needed.

Action planning: detailed work plans and budgets to implement the strategy. Draw up work plans and budgets on an annual basis to take into account progress made in implementing the strategy and resources available.

The idea of a rolling plan is that the mission is a longer-term and aspirational statement. It should give a permanent focus to the organisation.

The strategy will probably take a few years to pay off. All of the organisation's activities and resource allocations should fit with the strategy. The activity plan – budgets and work plans – can only really be estimated on an annual basis. The regular process of doing so is a chance to revisit the strategy and ensure that the organisation is still focused.

3   Assign responsibility

Identify and record which individuals and teams are responsible for different elements of the plan. This act of delegation needs to be a clear, public and negotiated one. Everyone needs to know who is responsible for different aspects of the strategy. Individuals to whom something is delegated must understand what is expected of them and feel that they have the authority, resources and organisational support to act.

4   Tight/loose

One popular management idea is to be tight on the ends, but loose on the means. The strategy should make it clear what the desired outcomes should be, but avoid being too prescriptive about the means or activity or tasks needed to achieve them. This gives staff the opportunity to develop work plans that are experimental, flexible and responsive in their content and methods, but still focused on achieving an outcome.

5   Build it into other processes

Once the strategy has been agreed it should feed into other managerial processes and be a reference point. For example, the strategy should influence staff training and development plans and individual work planning. Discussion about what the strategy means for each individual is a way of making it real. One organisation includes a section on 'contribution to the strategy' as a topic to be discussed in six-monthly review and appraisal meetings.

6   See the document as a road map

The document produced, be it called a strategic plan, business plan, forward plan or whatever, should be in a style that is active, concise and specific. It should make clear what is intended, how it will be done and give clear guidelines on how success should be measured and evaluated. If the document is too long or is written in an imprecise and vague way it will lose meaning and value.

7 Revisit assumptions

It is useful to record the main assumptions that you were operating to when you formulated the strategy. Examples of key assumptions might be:

'There will continue to be strong demand for our services'
'Public donations will continue at the same level'
'We will continue to be able to recruit and retain skilled volunteers'

Revisiting the assumptions can be revealing. If an assumption has proved not to be valid how might the strategy need changing? Are there any early signs that the assumption may not be correct?

8 Project change

A strategy needs to be more than a broad statement of goals and 'where you want to go'. All is in the detail of implementation. For major strategies it is useful to agree a separate implementation plan that should be managed as a 'change project'.

9 Fix the review process in advance

Often we forget to review things. A simple technique is to fix a review process at the start with clear time set aside in people's diaries or on meeting agendas to review milestones, review progress and update the strategy. The task of coordinating and leading this should be clearly assigned to an individual.

10 Acknowledge and share success

Nothing breeds success like success. Often people will renew their commitment to a new strategy if they can see it starting to pay off. The review process should look for examples of success, results and achievements. These should be shared in and around the organisation. Often in long-term strategies it is worthwhile to spot a few 'early wins' – things that show that the strategy is achieving something. Such examples of success show people that the strategy is still alive, is making progress and that people's work and effort is appreciated.

ORGANISATIONAL LEADERSHIP

Organisations are more than just a collection of structures, systems and procedures. How they operate more often than not depends upon how those in charge decide to play out their role and the kind of leadership managers give. It is possible to have an organisation with perfect policies and systems and with neat and tidy structures that is unproductive and unsuccessful. Management writers such as Peter Drucker have stressed the importance of distinguishing between being efficient and being effective.

This chapter looks at the question of leadership and the role of managers in not for profit organisations. It also describes the shift from managing to strategic leadership.

About leadership

In many not for profit agencies, 'Who is in charge?' is a difficult question to answer. In most organisations trustees or board directors have the final say and have a legal responsibility for the governance and proper management of the organisation. Most day-to-day management is delegated to paid staff. Often the relationship between boards and managers is confused and mutual expectations are not clearly agreed. In some organisations the issue of who is in charge causes conflict.

In some organisations management is still a new and even mistrusted idea. No one is quite sure what managers are meant to do – apart from be responsible for everything. In one advice agency a major decision was to rename the people who ran the advice centres from 'organisers' to 'managers'. Organisers were expected to do the work and ensure that the service operated to preset standards and procedures. The move to managers was seen as a positive way of recognising that the job was more than just organising or administration. It involved developing and coordinating internal and external relationships and building and controlling resources. It involved creating the basis for others to work effectively. The manager did not do the direct work – s/he supported and enabled those that did. In unhealthy organisations, however, management can become a thing in itself, taking resources away from the delivery of services and becoming disconnected from the organisation's users or front line staff. A danger sign is when managers speak an entirely different language from other staff.

Ten signs of an unhealthy organisation

1 The structures are top heavy

Too much time is spent on servicing the organisation (e.g. running internal meetings), as opposed to doing the work. Keeping the organisational structure serviced becomes a key and demanding job.

2 Systems do not work

There are regular breakdowns in the flow of information, decisions and feedback. Systems for communicating, making decisions, checking on progress and following up decisions often do not work.

3 Lack of unity of purpose

There is often confusion about what the organisation is for. People describe its purpose or vision differently or struggle to give a simple explanation of what its goals are.

4 Unresolved tensions and conflicts

There is a lack of a common ethos or shared values about how the organisation should operate. People have different views about what is important and how people should be treated.

5 Regular confusion about people's roles and expectations

The process for making a decision is confusing. People are mixed up about who is responsible and who has power.

6 Office politics dominate

Departments, teams and projects often clash with each other. The organisation is made up of several different power blocs that sometimes compete or battle against each other.

7 Led by crisis

There is no clear strategy or direction. The organisation is regularly bounced into things and fails to anticipate the need to change. Things only get done when they become a crisis.

8 No one knows what has been achieved

There is very little evaluation of what the organisation does. Work is only rarely studied to look for results, outcomes and impact. There is little organisational learning.

9 Communication does not happen

Communication gets blocked and people only find out things when it is too late. There is little effective dialogue or sharing of information and knowledge.

10 No development or learning

The organisation puts no real effort or resources into developing new ideas, activities and services. There is no time to think, innovate and experiment.

If you identify **all** ten factors as being relevant to your organisation ... then start looking around for another job ...

'Failing organisations are usually over-managed and under-led.'
– *Warren G. Bennis*

A stage on from management is leadership which can transform an unhealthy organisation. Leadership is a widely used word and often it implies that born leaders have some sort of super-human skills different from ordinary mortals. Leadership is not all about charisma and personality. It is about five things:

Focus: Ensuring that the organisation does not lose sight of its purpose and that the values of the organisation influence how it works. Managers who lead help people to see the bigger picture or context to their work. They focus on the ends as well as the means.

Taking your eye off the ball

A sports club appointed a new manager with ambitions and ideas. The manager set about developing plans for turning the old club house into a leisure centre with a gym, café and bar. The club's committee meetings were dominated by discussions of trading budgets, funding bids, architects' plans and other plans for the new buildings.

At the annual general meeting the committee reported on their hard work and plans. The discussion that followed was heated and critical. Members were concerned that the sporting performance of the club had declined, fewer younger people were participating and there was a shortage of volunteers to coach, organise and referee matches. Many members were unimpressed by the manager's hard work and ambitious projects. As one commented, 'This is meant to be a sports club – isn't it time we put our efforts into managing and developing sport rather than turning it into a social club?'.

After the meeting the manager realised that he had made a mistake in neglecting the core purpose and concentrating all his efforts on activities that were secondary to the main purpose.

Making sense of complexity: Our organisations can be confusing places. Different messages get given. People get pulled in different directions. Balancing the interests of users, funders, staff, volunteers, supporters and others can be a formidable task. Leaders need to understand such complexity and navigate a way through it.

Relationship management: Making people feel part of the organisation or building support for the organisation are critical jobs. Managers have to hold together a complex web of people who have different interests in the organisation. Some stakeholders might be internal ones such as staff and volunteers. They need to feel part of something and that their contribution makes a difference. External stakeholders might include funders, partners and supporters. They need to feel that their commitment or investment in the organisation is worthwhile.

Making strategy real: Managers who lead play a crucial role in formulating and implementing the organisation's strategy. They may lead or facilitate the discussions around the strategic process. A key role might be in helping others to understand the realities and external environment in which the organisation is operating. Once the strategy has been agreed their role will be to help the organisation to change to meet the strategy and ensure that the strategy is followed through.

Communication: Communication is more than sending out memos and e-mails. It is about helping people to understand what is happening in and around the organisation and to ensure that people are informed of progress. It is also about facilitating communication in the organisation – helping people to communicate and work together.

An impossible job?

Many not for profit organisations have an internal structure and way of operating that is vulnerable and shaky. A simple way of describing it is to draw it:

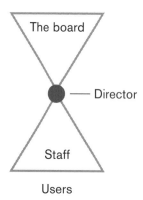

The board (or trustees or management committee) are the legal guardians of the organisation. They are responsible for ensuring that the organisation works in line with its aims and objectives. They appoint, direct and oversee the work of the Director and through them the staff of the organisation. The staff (paid and volunteer) carry out the work of the organisation and have most day to day contact with the users. The Director is at the centre of the model. S/he acts as the main channel of communication between the staff and the board. S/he advises on policy and strategy, oversees operations and is also often the main figurehead or representative of the organisation to the outside world.

This way of operating is common in many organisations, but despite this it is a precarious way of operating. A lot depends on the ability and skills of the person in the centre to hold it together and make it work. Several things can go wrong:

Only the Director sees the big picture. The Director sits in a pivotal position and is the only one who sees the whole picture. They understand how the organisation fits together and how policies, strategies and operational realities relate to each other. Others do not have such a broad and informed viewpoint so all thinking and planning about future development and strategy is abdicated to the Director.

People are kept in the dark. Board members only receive formal reports from the Director and lack any real feel for how the organisation actually works. Staff are so involved in delivering services that they lack any real involvement in the strategic and policy issues facing the organisation.

The Director becomes overloaded. The Director is pulled into playing too many roles. S/he struggles to balance advising the board, developing future strategies, building external relationships, managing the corporate centre and supervising staff and services. The Director jumps from role to role and after time either decides to ignore some roles or fails to be effective in any.

Relations and communication become strained. Communication becomes reactive. The Director communicates only on a 'need to know' basis. Board members only hear of a problem or issue when it becomes a crisis. Staff members only hear of policies after they have been decided. Some Directors have been known to 'play off' different groups against each other – Board members are told that their ideas will not work due to operational or staffing problems. Difficult or unpopular decisions are communicated to staff by the Director as being a decision made by the Board – despite the fact that the Director advised them to make it.

A question of style

How different managers operate and the way that they play out their leadership role can vary considerably, as this case illustrates:

Harry ran the Forrest Trust in a way that worked. Well, it worked for him! Harry saw his role as keeping all the different parts operating – but apart. The board of the trust was entirely dependent on Harry for information and advice. He produced or edited all reports and briefings that went to the board. Reporting back to the staff about the board was Harry's responsibility.

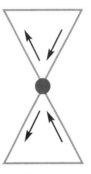 The staff were discouraged from taking too much interest in policy or strategic issues. Harry felt that making policy was his job – staff should be busy enough doing the day-to-day work.
Harry communicated on a need-to-know basis. He questioned the need to involve staff in discussions that were not their immediate concern. Harry liked to control the flow of information and communication around the organisation. He got annoyed when a board member started visiting the project unannounced. The board member wanted to show her interest and find out about the actual work of the organisation. Harry regarded the possibility of direct communication between board members and staff as potentially undermining his line management authority.

Due to an illness Harry took early retirement and was replaced by Kerry. Kerry soon realised that too much depended on her. The board had little feel for the organisation. The management and financial reports they received failed to convey any sense of the issues facing the trust's development. The board's meetings were very passive. The board had been encouraged to see their role as being to rubber stamp the manager's decisions or actions. It made no real independent contribution. The staff team worked hard, but had no real view of the bigger picture or external context facing the organisation. Few of the staff really understood how the organisation was funded. All management decisions were passed upwards for the manager to make. Staff complained about a lack of responsibility and that their ideas were not listened to.

Kerry set about changing this. She introduced a series of reforms. Board meetings were to have a two-stage agenda – a business part to report on organisational developments and a themed focus on an aspect of the trust's work. This discussion, led by a staff member or board member, would review

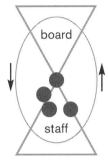

the background to the issue and raise options for the organisation. The board also set up two subgroups to review policies and coordinate the production of the strategic plan. Kerry reorganised the staff team to create three team leaders. After a planned programme of management development the team leaders would take on greater responsibility for running their aspect of the operation and playing a part in a management team.

After six months or so the Trust could point to a difference. The Board was much more informed and engaged in the organisation. It debated issues, helped to shape ideas for future developments and encouraged Kerry and the staff team to evaluate and develop their work. The staff team also began to change. There was much less dependence on the manager. Team leaders began to take responsibility for their work and became much more focused and responsible. Decisions were made faster.

One board member observed that a key change was a move from Harry's controlling style of leadership to Kerry's more facilitative one. Kerry developed people and opened up many of the processes and aspects of the organisation that in the past had been kept closed.

Making the structure work

Many organisations have developed processes and structures to avoid common problems and make management work. They include:

A management team: Staff supervised by the Director are encouraged to take more management responsibility. A management team is formed from the organisation's senior staff to be led by the Director. The team's role is to coordinate the work and make decisions or recommendations on corporate management issues. If the team works well, managers on it start to take responsibility for organisation-wide issues and not just the work of their unit.

An executive group: To involve the board more, the board's office holders (Chair, Treasurer etc.) meet on a regular basis with the Director and possibly the management team to process issues, check on the follow-up to decisions and take a strategic view. The Chair of an education charity that has used this idea describes it as 'working best when it is a sounding board for the Director. We have tried not to make decisions but rather identify issues and options for the full board. Or we have used the meeting as a monthly opportunity to stand back from issues and take stock'.

External support for the Director: To avoid the Director becoming isolated, arrangements are made for external support to be provided to them. This could include non-managerial supervision from a consultant, an arrangement where someone in a similar position acts as a mentor or where a board member agrees to provide regular contact and support. The purpose of these support arrangements is usually to help the Director review progress, reflect and discuss problems and to work on the Director's personal development.

Subgroups: A common approach is for the board to form subgroups that shadow the organisation's structure or services. These groups should give board members a greater understanding and feel for the issues facing the organisation and also increase the profile of the board within the organisation. They need clear terms of reference so that they do not undermine the board's role or confuse the internal management and supervisory relationships.

All of these ideas can work, but it is important that they are regularly reviewed and checked to ensure that they add value to the organisation and do not simply add more management or administration.

A strategic management approach

It is possible to make a distinction between strategic and operational management:

	Operational management	Strategic management
focus:	Day-to-day survival.	Long-term development of organisation.
objective:	Keeping things going as they are.	Finding better ways of doing things or exploring new ideas.
change:	Coping with imposed change.	Leading change.
motive:	Creating stability.	Creating future possibilities.
purpose:	Keeping current services functioning.	Exploring new services and ensuring future role.
process:	Use of procedures and systems.	Focus on evaluation, direction and vision.
decision making:	By precedent or rule book.	Considering future choices and options against strategy.

Operational management is important. It is about being efficient and ensuring that the organisation delivers and is reliable. Operational managers put emphasis on making sure that procedures and rules are in place to ensure that things happen as they are prescribed. They stress the importance of good organisation and systems.

Strategic management is about learning, evaluation, developing future ideas and change. Strategic managers are focused on future development and often spend time outside the organisation developing new ideas and projects. They are future orientated and are keen to see change as a continuous process of growth and learning.

It is not an either/or choice between operational or strategic managers. They both have positive or negative attributes. Operational managers can become bureaucratic and inflexible. They fail to respond to new needs or demands and think that if an answer is not in the rule book or manual then it does not exist. They are so involved in detail that they miss changes in the world outside. Strategic managers are sometimes criticised for being far too removed from operational realities. Their strategies lack practical application and fail to build on real life experience.

Linking strategy and action

Perhaps the best way forward is to have managers who can be effective both at operational and strategic management. Effective leadership involves both forms of management. The following four ideas are some of the ways that managers have tried to do this:

Link strategic thinking with operations. Many large organisations have created huge and powerful central policy or strategy functions that have churned out paper strategies for others to follow. This approach is now recognised as faulty. Ideas and strategies that work usually come from feedback from users or from people working with users. Strategic thinking needs to be informed by practical experience.

Build in evaluation throughout. Evaluation is about reviewing progress, identifying successes and failures, and learning. Good evaluation needs to be a regular process built into the organisation's way of working. It should not be seen as a 'bolt on' or something removed from real work.

Stand back. Often managers are too busy managing or coping with operational demands and crisis to be strategic. They become so involved in crisis management that they fail to see the cause or the solution. Managers need to be able to see their organisation from different perspectives and therefore must effectively manage their time and priorities.

Measure up/benchmark. A useful technique is to benchmark an aspect of your organisation against how it is performed in a similar organisation. The process of comparing can lead to many insights and also challenge complacency.

chapter 4

STRUCTURES – ORGANISING HOW YOU WORK

Structures should provide order, continuity and boundaries for our work and organisations. They should enable us to communicate internally and externally, respond to change and deliver work. They also are needed to ensure accountability and control the allocation of people's time and resources.

We can spend a lot of time trying to get our structures right. One voluntary organisation has a regular pattern whereby every three years it embarks on a reorganisation or a restructure. The organisational family tree gets dusted down, job descriptions get rewritten (often with upward salary regradings for those doing the rewriting), new teams are formed, but in reality everything stays the same – for the next three years. Coming up with ideas to change structures is easy – making the structure work is hard.

This chapter includes some ideas about how to develop organisational structures that fit with your organisation's purpose and strategy. It also covers different alternatives and options for designing organisations and shows you how to change and improve your organisation's structure.

Background of a typical organisation

Many of our organisational structures develop without much planning and thinking. Functions and people get added on as and when they appear and are needed. The structure is often a product of ad hoc developments or compromises between different interests.

Structures change as the organisation grows. A common pattern in many not for profit organisations is a four-stage one:

Early days: The organisation is informal, person centred and entrepreneurial in its style.

Expansion: Structures are established, management systems and procedures are brought in to cope with growth.

Consolidation: The emphasis is on procedures, control and bureaucracy.

Renewal: The organisation wants to be creative and get back in touch with the user. Teams and projects are used to encourage flexibility.

In the early days of a new organisation structures are often absent. Everything depends upon the ability of one or two key people to hold it all together. The key people (often the founder or first few workers) do everything and others support or back them up. They are too busy leading the organisation, raising its profile and raising money to spend time on structures.

As the organisation expands by taking on more work, moving into new areas and winning more resources, the ability of the key people to hold it together is challenged. The key people learn or through crisis are made to realise that they must delegate responsibility and create systems. They cannot do or oversee everything. Often external forces such as funders put pressure on the organisation to improve management. Structures are designed, teams or departments are formed, job descriptions get written and procedures for using resources are set in place.

After a process of expansion and growth the organisation needs to settle down. Management controls are brought in. Systems formalise how things work. There is sometimes a separation between those that deliver services to the user and those that manage, make strategies and control resources. This process of consolidation can lead to the organisation becoming remote, rigid and inflexible. Communication across the organisation is poor. The service user has to fit into the organisation rather than the organisation being able to fit in with the user.

The next stage, renewal, can often come about after a crisis (e.g. losing funding for a service) or changes in key personnel or pressure for the organisation to be more effective. Renewal can take the form of trying to make the organisation more flexible and responsive to its users or making it more able to deal with the rate of change in its external environment. Renewal might alternatively take the form of reducing the levels of controls of the centre or organisational core, empowering staff to make more decisions and creating a more flexible, team based structure.

Reasons to review your structure

1 **Overload and underload**
   The allocation of work and responsibilities is not reasonable and logical. Some people or teams have too much to do and some parts of the organisation are underused.

2 **Overlaps cause confusion and conflict**
   The boundaries between people or team responsibilities do not make sense. Often it is not clear who is responsible for a task.

3 **Confused reporting lines**
   People are not clear to whom they are accountable.

4   Uncertainty about responsibilities

Responsibilities for controlling resources and budgets and the management of work are vague and can cause conflict.

5   Long-term poor performance

You suspect that the way the organisation is organised might be a major reason why the organisation or a key part of it fails to meet its target or to perform to plan.

6   New priorities and demands

A change in direction means that the organisation has to be organised differently to meet new users, changing expectations and new work.

7   The structure is blocking your strategy

You suspect that the way that you are organised is a major hindrance to achieving your strategy.

When not to do it

1   As a quick fix

Often managers focus in on the structure rather than dealing with more difficult and complex issues. Sometimes it is easier to play around with the organisation's structure chart than to work out a strategy or direction.

2   To show that you are in charge

It is not unknown for new managers or directors to 'do a reorganisation' as a way of stamping their name on the organisation. In the reorganisation they can reward loyal supporters and reduce the status of troublesome individuals.

3   To reorganise a problem

Rather than deal with an individual's poor performance and their inability to work as part of a team, one manager devised a whole new organisational structure to manage around one 'problem' individual.

Types of structures

Management text books offer no shortage of models and theories of how to organise. Three are particularly common:

Functional organisation: People are grouped together by skills or profession. Finance staff are all in one unit, care workers in another. Units are usually led by people from that function.

Divisional: The agency organises itself around particular outputs or services. Mini organisations or 'business units' are formed to work on and deliver a particular service or product.

Matrix: In a matrix organisation teams or project groups are formed with people from different functional groups to do a particular job. The arrangements last for as long as the project is needed. People from different functional groups must learn ways of working together.

One housing association worked all three of these designs. When it started out it seemed logical to group staff in a functional structure based around housing management, finance, development, maintenance and administration. Each department was headed by a manager who together with the Director formed a senior management team.

The advantages were that:

- The structure encouraged technical expertise.
- It created a career structure – people could move up their functional ladder.
- It encouraged good supervision and support – managers knew the jobs that they were managing.

After a while disadvantages became clear:

- It was not conducive to team work and good customer care, as people were regularly shunted back and forth between one department and another and no one took responsibility for the whole problem.
- It encouraged people to have a narrow perspective.

The association then decided to move towards a decentralised divisional structure based around a central office and four local offices. The local area offices were to have all the functions necessary to run and develop services in their locality. Local managers were instructed to manage the whole service in their areas. The central office would contain management service functions, such as central accounts and personnel and some functions such as architects, that it did not make practical sense to devolve to the areas.

The main gains with this structure were that:

- The local managers were accountable for all aspects of performance in their area – they could not blame a problem on another department.
- In some instances team working improved.
- Responsiveness and decision making was faster as local managers had a clear sense of their responsibilities for their area.

Over time, problems set in. The local areas became mini-organisations and resented the involvement of the head office. The organisation found it harder and harder to justify the costs involved in running the head office given that it mainly consisted of administrative and internal management costs. It was interesting to note that gradually, functional organisation crept back in. The headquarters finance controller acted as if she line-managed the area finance officers who on paper reported to the local managers.

A new strategy for the association, of being involved in building strong local communities and playing a part in urban regeneration, has led to a move to a matrix structure. To develop and bid for funds to run projects, teams from across the organisation are assembled. Flexible project structures are used to deliver short-term initiatives. As well as having functional and local responsibilities many staff are also working on and leading project teams and task forces.

Working in a matrix structure is challenging. The organisation is constantly forming and reforming as and when the work requires. Often staff have to manage having two or even three bosses and being answerable to their line manager and to the leaders of project or task groups.

Reviewing their experience of functional, divisional and matrix working the association's Director commented:
'No one structure works well all the time. It's very much horses for courses. You have to make sure that the structure helps the organisation to deliver rather than holds it back. There is a real responsibility for managers to help people be effective in whatever structure you have and to recognise how the structure is developing.'

Under new management

Several factors are making voluntary and not for profit organisations question how they structure organisations. Factors include:

A fast rate of external change: Many organisations have to find quick and effective ways of responding to new initiatives, policy directions and funding opportunities. Organisations cannot afford to be too rigid. The structure needs to be open and flexible enough to take on new initiatives.

Projects rather than core: Often it is easier to get funding for projects rather than core or permanent activities. Many organisations are a collection of fixed-term funded projects supported by an organisational centre or core.

Need for new services: Organisations have to continually develop new services and activities. Innovation and creativity need to be built into the organisation's structure. Evaluation and learning from experience becomes a key attribute upon which to build progress.

Concerns about risk and governance: Managers and trustees have to find ways of managing short-term flexibility.

OLD IDEAS   **NEW IDEAS**

Permanent  Flexible

Structures were traditionally designed to last and be fixed. Now flexibility needs to be built into structures so that new work can develop. A core structure is needed that can provide continuity and stability, but it must be able to act as a framework for short-term projects and new work.

Single function  Multi-skilled

Organising people in functional groups made sense when staff needed minimal communication and joint working. Increasingly people from different professional or occupational groups are being organised together to break down traditional barriers and create more 'joined up' services.

Complex and highly   Flatter structures
layered

Traditionally organisational structures had several levels in the hierarchy: Director, Deputy Director, Managers, Team Leaders, senior workers, operational staff and support staff. Recently many organisations have reduced the number of levels in the hierarchy to improve communication between policy and operational managers and to reduce the levels of bureaucracy and overhead costs.

Job descriptions  Flexible job roles
highly defined

In an attempt to cover every possibility, job descriptions are often an exhaustive list of all possible tasks. They are often written to get a salary grade. Tightly defined job descriptions can lead to demarcation problems and disputes over responsibilities and expectations. An alternative is to see job design as a moving picture rather than a fixed one. People should be recruited with a variety of skills that can be used and developed in the organisation. A job description needs to describe the work, outline the results and outcomes, but recognise that the job will change.

Central control of all   Much more delegation
resources   and devolution of
                                                 power and resources

Increased use of technology and a commitment to empower people has led to many organisations delegating budget control from the centre to local managers. Local managers are encouraged to use their resources to meet needs and objectives as they see fit, rather than being told how they can spend their project or service money by their head office.

Uniform employment      Variety of employment
conditions   systems arrangements

Traditionally people were employed on a standard contract with little flexibility. In many workplaces there is now a variety of employment arrangements available. Some people work on full-time permanent contracts; others on fixed-term contracts; on job share arrangements; term-time only contracts; freelance contracts; or seconded from other employers. The organisation's structure and systems need to be flexible enough to accommodate a variety of people working in different ways.

Functions provided   Outsourcing or buying
in house   in expertise as needed

Rather than employing people directly and adding on functions as the organisation grows, many organisations now outsource or contract in functions as and when they are needed. The service is provided to contract by an outside expert company or casual staff. Examples of outsourcing include fundraising, training, computer support, marketing, research as well as support functions such as cleaning, catering and building management.

Inside or out – about outsourcing

A significant business trend has been to buy in services and activities on a contract basis rather than to employ people to do them in-house on a permanent basis. Some examples include:

In a period of rapid expansion a voluntary organisation negotiated agreements with external companies to provide a management services function: payroll, accounts and building management. The alternative would have been to employ an administrator to cover a wide variety of management and organisational tasks.

A housing project restructured its management team. It did away with the full-time post of Deputy Director and replaced it with three associates covering personnel, technology and fundraising. The associates were guaranteed a set number of days per month. Three individuals were recruited with specialist skills and were assigned projects by the Director.

A charity decided to contract out certain headquarters functions such as training, marketing and design and the management of its website. Contracting services out to freelancers, consultants and other organisations opened up access to a range of skills and experiences that it could never have in one job.

Advocates of outsourcing would argue that it has the following advantages:

It is a cost effective way of bringing in expertise
An organisation can negotiate a variety of arrangements with independent expert suppliers to tailor the service for them.

You only pay for it when you need it
Having a service as a variable cost rather than a fixed cost can make financial sense. If you set up a function or service on a permanent basis there is a risk that for some of the time it will not be needed. With some outsourcing arrangements you only have to pay for a service when you need it.

It allows the organisation flexibility
Using outsourcing allows you to grow or shrink quickly. Rather than having to make a risky decision to employ permanent staff, outsourcing a task or function might be a suitable way to cope with growth.

You focus on managing your core expertise
Often managers spend more time managing the periphery of their organisation rather than their core business. The Director of a training

agency complained that he spent more time crisis managing the centre's canteen than developing its training programme. Outsourcing allows you to focus on what is critical to your organisation.

It is easier to measure performance
Contract reviews and performance measures all mean that there are in-built mechanisms to ensure that the outsourced service is delivering and that it is being evaluated. In-house permanent functions often lack such measures.

It stops the core of the organisation from being bureaucratic and top heavy
Outsourcing makes it clear how much management and support functions are costing. Such information might help people to question their value in the workplace and ensure that they are contributing.

Critics of outsourcing would put forward the following arguments against it:

It can reduce employment security
Outsourcing arrangements are often brought into an organisation to cut costs and jobs. Outsourced contracts usually mean temporary and short-term contracts for employees.

It removes expertise from within the organisation
There is a risk that by transferring functions from in-house to outside suppliers knowledge and expertise is lost. One organisation moved away from outsourcing when its managers realised that none of its staff knew the detail of its computer system. They were totally reliant on outside suppliers.

It can be more expensive
The outside supplier has to charge a fee that covers their full costs and includes a contribution to their overheads and profit targets as well as covering time that they are not working.

The organisation lacks flexibility
By moving functions and services to outside suppliers organisational flexibility and responsiveness is lost. If something goes wrong or is unexpected it has to be covered by the contract or involve an additional payment to the supplier.

Design decisions

In designing or redesigning your organisation the following four issues should be considered:

What to organise around

What should be the building blocks of the organisational structure? Various possibilities can be considered:

Points of delivery – Many organisations are structured around the location of services and geography. For example a care organisation structured its work into twenty local branches in turn supervised by three areas.

Types of work/client – An alternative is to structure your organisation around the kind of functional work that you do (for example youth work/ training/advice etc) or the type of client (for example, services to children).

Contract/business or income – One increasing trend is to link the structure to funding or income streams: projects are created and added to the structure that link directly to a contract or funding agreement.

Span of control

How many people, activities and types of work can one individual manager supervise efficiently? If the number of people reporting to an individual increases or the range of their direct supervisory responsibilities grows beyond a reasonable level there is a strong possibility that mistakes may get made and management becomes entirely reactive.

User's perspective

An interesting exercise is to try to look at the organisation from 'outside – in'. If the organisation were redesigned around the user needs, expectations and likes, what would it look like? How would they access services? How would you ensure that they did not spend time being passed around from team to team? Who would manage or oversee their 'journey' through the organisation?

Authority and responsibility

How should power and decision making be allocated? What checks and balances need to be built in? Should authority and power be held and controlled centrally by a few key people or should power be devolved and delegated?

The centre

One of the most lively debates in organisational development is about the relationship between the organisational centre or headquarters and the services and projects.

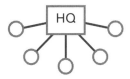 As organisations grow it is usual for an administrative and managerial function to evolve that is separate from the direct services. This administrative and managerial function often becomes a central office or headquarters.

In many organisations controversies can occur about the role of the centre. Managers described some of the problems:

'In my organisation the central office adds on a 16% management fee to any project bid to cover a contribution to central office costs. It isn't just the funders who are questioning this fee. My projects get very little back in terms of useful support and help. The central office just gobbles up management fees to keep itself going.'

'Our head office just keeps on growing. They keep developing new systems and creating more work for us. As the organisation has grown, a distance has developed between the head office and the people doing the real work. They talk in one language. We talk in another.'

Three particular issues can cause trouble:

Some funding bodies are reluctant to pay for non-service costs
Some funders take the view that they should fund only direct service delivery and not management overheads. One agency found it relatively easy to win support for project funding, but very hard to generate income to pay for the organisational infrastructure.

Power struggles
Often there is a difficult relationship between the organisational centre and the teams and units that have most to do with the organisation's user. The centre is seen as a weight on the organisation. It ties local managers up in procedures and systems and seems intent on making their life harder. Policies are passed down from on high with little understanding of the realities of operational life.

Status and values
In many organisations and careers the more contact that you have with the user the less you get paid. Career paths take people away from the user and into management or strategic roles that have little direct contact. It is as if the real status and reward comes from being in the head office.

Changing the centre

The following four points are some ideas designed to create a more productive and effective relationship:

Make the centre add value

The organisational centre should see its role as adding value to the organisation rather than taking value away. The centre should 'earn its keep'. It is possible to identify several ways in which an organisational centre can add value:

Through providing quality assurance

Through providing support, training and supervision

Through providing back up and support

By bringing in extra funding to enhance services

By providing an effective management and administrative support.

The centre as a supporter rather than a controller

It is very easy for an organisational centre to fall into a command and control approach to management. The centre issues orders and commands to be followed by local staff. An alternative model is where the centre sees its role as helping and supporting local managers. A personnel officer in a national agency described how she saw her role:

'There are two ways I could play my role. The easy way would be to sit in the head office devising new procedures and policies for local managers to follow. My job would then be to enforce the rules and check up on local managers. The other approach is to see my role as supporting local managers in personnel matters. My role is to act as an internal consultant and coach rather than a controller or head office enforcer.'

Move away from top-down policy making

Some organisations have tried to move away from a centralised or top-down approach to policy making. Often organisations create divides between those who make policy and those who implement it. Such divisions create tensions and conflicts. Seeing policy and strategy making as a participative process means involving staff early, before policy is made rather than as an afterthought. Using project teams and task forces, and encouraging ideas for future policy development to come from operational staff are all ways of breaking down communication barriers, which should lead to a successful policy that has a better chance of implementation.

Measure and manage the centre's contribution

Organisations should occasionally evaluate and review what contribution and value the organisational centre makes. Questions to consider might include:

Who are the centre's customers?
What do people think of the centre's services?
Is the cost of the centre fair?

One idea now common in parts of the public sector is for the centre and projects to agree internal service agreements setting out what the centre will do and what projects and services can expect. Such agreements make the centre's contribution much more tangible and clear.

Managing structures

Managers should also consider the following three points about structures:

Few organisational structures work perfectly all of the time. They need reviewing to check that they perform well and occasionally evaluating to ensure that processes happen as intended.

Whilst structures should be checked once in a while, resist the temptation to *continually* review and change the structure. Changing structures can create an illusion of progress, but often once the structure has settled into place the same problems occur. Structures are only one part of creating an effective organisation. Other issues such as strategy, people's performance and leadership are just as crucial – but possibly harder to deal with.

There is a paradox about working flexibly. Increasingly managers talk about empowerment and encouraging flexibility and initiative amongst staff. Some of the more intrusive controls are being scrapped. Experience would suggest that in order to work flexibly and have independence and initiative people need clear boundaries, discipline and useful control and support systems. Without such structure they sink, but the right balance of order and flexibility brings out the best in people.

How technology can change how we work

Developments in information and communication technology can also change many of the ways in which we organise and structure work. For benefits to be realised, managers must think about how best to use technology in the design of organisational systems and processes. Here are some examples of the ways in which the application of information and communication technology can change how organisations work.

Work flexibly

Technology has the potential to enable people to work differently. Some staff can work from home or other more local locations and still be in touch with the organisation.

Boundaries disappear

Technology can make communication faster and enable people to work together over a distance. One campaigning organisation has started using telephone and video conferencing to enable campaign teams to stay in touch on a weekly basis without the cost and time involved in holding national meetings.

Knowledge management

Internal internet systems, intranets, can mean that all staff can access information and data. Organisations can use such systems to build up resource banks of practical information, past work and contacts. Such systems protect and share out the organisation's collective 'know how'.

Information for all

Technology gives the potential for much greater openness and transparency in the flow of information within the organisation. Effective management can mean that most information becomes more open and accessible. Staff can find out information for themselves rather than having to wait until managers decide to communicate.

ORGANISATIONS WORKING TOGETHER – FROM ALLIANCES TO MERGERS

This chapter looks at something which should be straightforward – how to get organisations that are committed to the same or similar purpose to work together either through informal means or through formal structures. It should be straightforward, but it often is not. Getting organisations to share things and cooperate can be hard work and fraught with difficulties.

This chapter looks at four issues:

- Why should organisations work together?
- Some forms and structures to enable organisations to work together
- Common blocks and barriers
- Some ideas on how the process can be encouraged

Why do it?

There are many different reasons for considering working together. Some reasons are short-term, others are more fundamental:

1 Other people do the same thing consistently better

It might be that you recognise that other organisations are more effective than you. Working closely with them or deciding to merge with them might be a way of ensuring that the quality of your work improves.

2 Costs are too high

Often people look at working together as way of combating duplication, reducing overhead costs and achieving more with the same resources. Sometimes a direct saving can be shown. For example a group of five community care agencies decided to set up a consortium to run staff development and training for all their staff. This was significantly cheaper than all five agencies having to set up an in-house training function. However there are some anecdotal reports of costs in larger merged organisations rising as the organisation has to take on more administrative costs.

3 Competition is destructive

Coming together in alliances or in one organisation is one well used technique to overcome competition for resources and funds.

4 Organisational divisions don't make sense

Often the way in which organisational boundaries operate is a product of ad hoc development and peculiar circumstances. In one small town an unemployed person with children needed to make contact with six different agencies to get careers advice, get advice on student financial support, find and enrol on a college course and find a nursery place. Moving to a 'one-stop shop' approach might make services more accessible and more holistic from the user point of view.

5 Being alone is no longer viable

In some instances the costs of being independent might not make sense. A one-worker health project was alarmed to find that up to 40% of its staff time was being spent on running the organisation (servicing the management committee, doing fundraising and financial management) as opposed to delivering services. Moving into a similar organisation would mean that some administrative functions could be shared and create more time for the core purpose.

6 Added value: The belief that 2+2 might = 5

Through combining resources it may be possible to create a synergy, where the combination of the parts is greater together than being apart. Two organisations that merged found that they achieved added value in their fundraising. One organisation had real strengths in winning corporate sponsorship and the other had developed effective ways of raising money from supporters. Combining expertise and relevant strengths should add value.

7 External forces press for it

Increasingly some funders are complaining of there being too many organisations and of duplication. One local authority director remarked, 'We have seven different organisations all struggling to run day centres and OAP luncheon clubs. They all have the same problems. Surely it would be much better (and possibly cheaper) if they came together in one structure?'. It is worth noting that the same authority makes public statements about the need for a diversity of provision.

How to do it?

Often any discussion of working closely together is immediately seen as an intention to merge into one single organisation. This next section looks at ten possible organisational forms that can enable organisations to work together. Most of them would not involve any legal change or permanent structural change.

Joint management of a project

Description: Sharing in creating and managing a new service.

Issues: In this arrangement organisations come together to start and run a project as a joint venture. Often it is useful if one of the organisations acts as lead body and carries out legal and employment responsibilities. It is worthwhile to have some written agreement setting out the responsibilities of all parties in the venture.

Sharing of overheads and costs

Description: Sharing offices, staff time and running costs.

Issues: Organisations agree to share certain functions in order to save or reduce running costs. This is a useful way of helping to reduce costs as an organisation grows and as such is often a temporary measure. A written agreement should be drawn up to help resolve and avoid disputes.

Housing a project

Description: An established organisation agrees to house a new project rather than the new project having to set up an independent organisation with its own legal structure.

Issues: The project operates as part of the parent organisation and as such is a full constituent part of it. This can be a useful way of quickly starting a new project as the project should enjoy the stability of the established parent organisation. Usually the project will be charged a management fee by the parent organisation.

Consortium

Description: Several agencies combine together to set up an organisation to carry out a particular function.

Issues: If several organisations all recognise that they have a particular need, then forming a consortium to meet that need may be an effective option. The consortium may in itself be an independent body with people from the founding bodies represented on its board.

Alliance

Description: Organisations with a particular interest coming together to campaign.
Issues: Organisations agree to form a common 'front' to coordinate, lead and focus their campaigning work. Alliances are often short lived and work best when there is a specific issue that can create a unity between organisations.

Referral routes

Description: Organisations agree how to 'route' clients between agencies. Agencies agree which organisation will specialise on particular clients or issues.
Issues: Trying to map out services so that they all fit together can lead to this process. It is often interesting to look at the journey that users have had to follow to get to a service.

Territory agreement

Description: An informal or even formal agreement about which organisation will lead or deliver services in a particular area.
Issues: The intention is to stop wasteful competition and empire building. Difficult to police or enforce.

Managing agent

Description: One organisation agrees to manage an activity or service on behalf of the other.
Issues: A sub-contracting relationship. This type of arrangement is common in special needs housing, where a housing association works with a voluntary agency to provide accommodation. Usually this arrangement has a written agreement setting out responsibilities and expectations.

Outsourcing

Description: An organisation contracts out a function or task to another organisation to perform on its behalf. For example, one agency might agree that another organisation might manage on its behalf its transport service.
Issues: Outsourcing often happens if the organisation feels that another organisation can manage and deliver the function better than they can.

Merging

Description: Organisations join together to form a new organisation.
Issues: Parties to the merger come together to create a new body involving the transfer of services, assets and staff to the new merged body. Some mergers are a takeover, where a bigger or stronger organisation takes over a smaller or weaker one.

Why joint working sometimes fails

Here are four common issues that block joint working:

Ego

Working together requires cooperation and a willingness to put the common goal above the needs of individual organisations. However, ego can get in the way. Some directors or trustees like being in charge of 'their show' and despite their rhetoric find cooperation, sharing and having to work with others a problem.

Minor sticking points grow

Joint ventures sometimes come unstuck because a relatively small issue is not dealt with and blocks cooperation. In one joint project between two environmental organisations the project staff team was made up from employees of both parties. As people worked together, differences in pay grade, holiday entitlement and working conditions began to cause disunity in the staff group. A failure to resolve these issues meant more time was spent by the project group and by the two organisations on personnel issues than on the strategy for the project.

The process drags on

The process for putting joint ventures together can be an arduous one. People have to report back to their organisations and ensure that they as representatives and negotiators have support. It is worthwhile mapping out a timetable for setting up the joint project and ensuring that there is adequate time for proposals to go back to each party for consideration and approval. The process needs planning and synchronising and possibly independent facilitation.

Competition beats cooperation

Often competition feels attractive. Managers find themselves in situations where they believe they can achieve more by looking after their own interests. In one situation the main voluntary providers of community care agreed to work together as a consortium to negotiate service level agreements. The arrangement fell apart as two of the organisations broke ranks to negotiate their own agreement. One of the participants, reflecting on the issues, commented, 'At a policy level everyone signed up to working cooperatively, but when it came to sharing information on things like project costings some members of the group fell away. They could not shift their mindset from playing games to cooperation'.

The process – making it happen

Creating joint working between organisations demands careful negotiation, clear and assertive communication and openness about potential problems. The following process is a decision guide:

1 Start with the big picture

Discussions that explore joint working should start by identifying either how the user may benefit from any joint venture or how working together could enable both organisations to achieve more. All too often discussions about joint working get too concerned too early with how to make structures and staff roles fit together. Start by looking at what value could be added and then go onto the detail of how to do it. Three techniques are helpful in doing this:

Future scan for possible scenarios: Spend time looking at how user needs might develop and how external factors might affect your work. Would greater cooperation be a sound strategy? If you worked together could there be a definite gain?

Collaborate over strategic and business planning: One idea is to link the process of strategic planning between different organisations. As organisations consult with each other on their future plans and priorities areas of possible cooperation might become obvious.

Draw agency/service maps: A simple and often revealing exercise is to draw a map of the different services available to the user. Does the map make sense? Are there areas of over-supply and gaps in provision? If agencies worked closer together could the user get a better deal?

2 Review possible forms of joint working

The next stage in the process is to look at what possible formats for cooperation are available. Several issues will have impact on the kind of structure chosen:

Short-term/long-term need

If the issues that have put potential cooperation on the agenda are short-term then the structural format should be flexible, project based and easy to bring to an end. Possible formats might include joint management of a project, an alliance or a managing agent relationship. If the issues are longer-term then the format needs to be more permanent and provide the venture with a degree of stability. Longer-term forms of cooperation are consortia and mergers.

The level of 'fit' between agencies

An important issue to explore is how well the organisations will fit together. It is worthwhile spending time letting each party learn about the other – a courting phase. The chair of trustees of a voluntary project described how their cooperation/merger talks fell apart: 'Both organisations were of similar size, with the same client group and similar services. On paper it looked like a perfect fit. When we started talking it became clear that we operated to a very different philosophy and also had very different organisational cultures. We decided to stay apart – rather than force a merger.'

Issues of identity and independence

Working together can be hard work. In the early stages a joint venture might be seen as taking more than it gives. In some forms of cooperation such as consortia, alliances and mergers, people may see the independence, autonomy and separate identity of their organisation being reduced in the interests of the joint venture. Are people prepared for that to happen?

3 Clear, transparent and assertive negotiations

It is important that parties agree a process that works for discussing issues. The process needs to involve all of the organisations and ensure that people are kept informed throughout. Sometimes it is useful to engage a consultant or independent person to facilitate and steer the process. Another approach is for each organisation to appoint people to a team to manage the process.

It is important to have clear agreement on how staffing matters in any joint venture should be dealt with. Staff need to know who their employer is and who they are accountable to for line management and supervision.

In most instances it is worth recording the nature of the agreement and the roles and responsibilities of all parties in the venture. Legal advice may be needed to draw this up. A useful exercise is for all parties to explore worst-case scenarios and indulge in a game of 'what ifs?', e.g. 'How would a dispute about priorities for the project be resolved?'.

Working together – steering the process

Many attempts to encourage organisations to work together fail. The City Connections Agency is an established voluntary organisation providing training and support to young people. The agency's Director, Rachel, described the organisation's experience of one unsuccessful and one successful attempt to work collaboratively with other organisations.

A series of informal contacts with Skillsbase, a local vocational training provider, led to a protracted and drawn out series of discussions about a possible merger. Rachel and the Manager of Skillsbase discussed the possible benefits of combining staff and buildings and operating as one centre. They drafted a confidential paper for both their management committees that looked at how a single operation would reduce administrative cost and put the organisation in a stronger position to win contracts and pursue new opportunities. Rachel commented on how both organisations reacted to the idea. 'People immediately became involved in the detail. Budgets were scrutinised. Potential anomalies in pay gradings and employment terms were discussed in detail. This produced a defensive and uncreative approach to discussions and joint contact. Many people saw the issue as being "which organisation was taking over the other one". At no stage did we ever sit down and discuss how joint working and a merger could benefit our users. Eventually both parties lost interest and were unable to summon up energy to overcome the blocks. After a few months the idea quietly died away.'

A year later a former board member of the agency contacted Rachel to see if the agency and her project could work closely together. Her project worked with young people leaving care and had particular expertise with young women. This time Rachel and her colleague tackled the opportunity differently. To ensure that everyone was involved they convened a joint meeting of staff and board members to explore ways of working together. The meeting looked at the respective strengths and skills of both organisations. It explored common values and ethos and discussed how possible ways of working together could improve services. The meeting was positive – it led to a couple of small examples of cooperation between staff. One of the agency's staff offered to help the project look into accreditation of its training courses. A joint steering group was set up to explore possibilities.

The steering group reported back with the recommendation to merge both organisations and create a new organisation. To reassure staff, pledges were given to meet legal obligations to honour contracts as well as a full commitment to involve all staff in the process of planning the merger.

The joint steering group managed the task of creating a new and merged organisation. The merger was a success. The two organisations complement each other and the merger is generally regarded by staff and users as a positive thing.

Rachel draws three main conclusions from the process:

1   Throughout the process it is critical to focus on what value and benefit any arrangement could bring to the user or beneficiaries of the organisation. Increasing benefit and value should be the driving force.

2   Detail has its place, but minor details can slow down and even derail the process. Organisations need to agree how to resolve issues of detail and delegate the task of doing so.

3   Rather than cobbling two organisations together it is better to see it as creating a new one. Such a position opens up possibilities, allows flexibility and creativity and reduces allegations of one organisation taking over another.

ORGANISATIONAL PROJECTS

This chapter suggests how organisations can use projects, task groups or working groups to achieve short-term tasks. It introduces a project management approach that can be used in planning and managing a range of tasks and activities within an organisation. Examples of projects include:

- Bringing staff together to work on an organisation-wide problem or issue such as designing and bringing in a new computer system
- Running a campaign
- Devising and implementing a new policy
- Carrying out an organisational task such as a reorganisation

The chapter outlines a framework for project management and describes some tools and approaches organisations can use.

Why create a project?

Increasingly organisations are sorting work into projects. Staff are assigned to work on a project for a fixed time period to achieve a definite result. Projects – when they work well – are a useful way of allocating resources to a particular issue or problem and providing a focus to it. The individuals involved are given the responsibility for delivering the project in line with the requirements and expectations set at the start.

Creating project teams to do specific work has many advantages:

A multi-disciplinary approach

Creating a project team can bring a variety of different skills and experience to a problem. The project team can have on it people with a range of skills and perspectives that no one individual will have.

Projects create focus and urgency

By designating something as a project it can stress the importance of an issue to the organisation. It gives notice that a special effort is being made to work on an issue to a set timetable. Project working stresses the importance of delivering clear results.

Responsibilities are clear

In establishing a project it becomes clear who is responsible for a particular issue or task. Good project working makes clear to whom tasks are assigned. They know what is expected of them. The rest of the organisation knows what they are responsible for delivering, and accountability is increased.

Individuals can learn and develop

By working on a project an individual may get responsibilities that are different from or greater than their usual day-to-day job. This can provide a useful way of learning new insights and skills.

What is special about projects?

The following five issues make project management different and as such require a different set of skills and approaches.

A project only lasts for a fixed time

Projects are not permanent. Often when you start on a project the only thing that is clear is when the project has to deliver by and thereby end. Managing a fixed-term piece of work requires planning, discipline and an ability to start at the end and work backwards.

A project is unique – it is a one-off

Projects must respond to specific circumstances and needs. The brief for the project will pose problems and detail needs. The project should be creative in how it solves and addresses them, and be innovative in its design and execution. It should not just copy what has been done before.

A project involves and depends upon others

Projects are not one-person shows. They must involve other people in their design, delivery and follow-up. The project leader has to find ways of involving people in the project's design, keeping people in touch with progress and also be able to hand it over when the project is wound up.

A project creates change

Although the project is temporary and fixed-term it should be able to produce something that lasts. The project's product might be quite tangible, such as a new information system or a reorganisation, or it might be more intangible, such as a new working practice. Project leaders need to be skilled in planning and managing change.

A project is performance orientated

Projects usually have defined goals and aims. Working on a project is often more task focused than working in a permanent job or function. It is easier to judge if a project has been a success or failure.

A framework for projects

Often organisations set up projects in a 'half hearted' way: expectations are not clear; roles are not established; people drift into and out of the project. Here is how one worker in a charity described her experience:

> 'Our new chief executive decided that our internal communications systems needed overhauling. No one knew what was happening. After discussions at the staff conference I was appointed to lead a project team to "come up with ways of improving communication". Three other staff were "volunteered" to work with me.

> 'We spent the first two meetings trying to work out what was expected of us. We had no structure or plan to work to. We also had our normal jobs to do. After the third meeting I wrote a report with the ideas and recommendations that we had scraped together and presented it to the Chief Executive.

> 'A few days later they told me that the report had addressed different issues than the ones intended. How was I supposed to have known? The report was quietly forgotten about. I have never been asked or volunteered to lead any other project since!'

One of the reasons why projects can go wrong is that they need to work across the traditional boundaries, structures and processes of the organisation. The project is added onto the organisation. A useful model for managing projects sees an organisational project as having six elements:

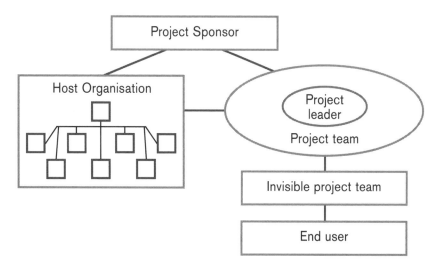

Who is who?

The project sponsor

The project sponsor is the person or body (e.g. management committee) who has the status and power over resources to give authority to the project's establishment. The project may be their idea or an idea that they have chosen to back. They will set or approve the brief for the project, appoint the project leader and ensure that the project has the resources and organisational support to do the job.

The project leader

The project leader or project manager is the individual responsible for the successful implementation and delivery of the project. The project may be their full-time job or it may be one of several responsibilities in their job. The project leader should see the project through from start-up to completion.

The host organisation

The host organisation houses the project. The project is added or superimposed onto the structures and work of the permanent organisation. Members of staff may be appointed or seconded to work on the project. The host organisation will continue after the project closes.

The project team

Rather than asking the project leader to do all the work, often a project team is established to work with the project leader on delivering the project. The project team members will work on the project as well as carrying out their usual duties.

The invisible project team

This interesting idea comes from work carried out by Briner, Geddes and Hastings in their work at Ashridge Management College. The invisible project team are individuals and groups who have a stake or interest in the project. For the project to succeed the cooperation and backing of these people is critical. Some of the invisible project team might be people who have power or influence to determine if the project will be a success. Others might be people who you need to work with or through to be successful. Often the invisible project team are the people who will be needed to carry the work on after the project has ended.

The end users

The end users are the people who should benefit from the project. In a technology project the end users might be the staff who will use the new computer system. The end users of a project to devise a new policy would be the staff and volunteers expected to carry it out.

This is quite a complex model for an organisational project. It is more than just a structural map. It also highlights several points of conflict and tensions that project leaders need to be aware of. Three common ones are:

A conflict between the host organisation and the project

Often people in the host organisation see the project as grabbing all the interesting work and taking resources away from the day-to-day work. One unit head of a housing association complained that, 'My best staff are constantly being stolen to work on organisation-wide projects. The projects always take more time than was intended, so their permanent work suffers. The projects have all the status and profile in the organisation, yet it is the units that do the real day-to-day work'.

A conflict between the project sponsor's expectations and those of the end users

Often senior people sponsor projects based on the slimmest knowledge of what is actually needed by the user. Projects are devised with very little input from the user. One manager described how in their organisation projects were often set up after the Director had been to a conference, learnt a few new buzz words, pinched other people's ideas and decided that 'we will do that'. When the project delivers, the director has lost interest and moved onto other things. Users are frustrated because something is delivered that is not wanted. The project leader, rather than the project sponsor, gets the blame.

A conflict between the project sponsor and the line management of the host organisation

Often project leaders feel pulled between their project sponsor and their line manager. They have to operate in two systems. Often resources and time leak from the organisation to the project. The project leader has to ensure that the host organisation is kept in touch with project developments and that the project sponsor is prepared to pick up any extra work involved when the project ends.

The life cycle of a project

Many of these conflicts can be resolved through better project management and design. Most organisational projects work through various stages or phases:

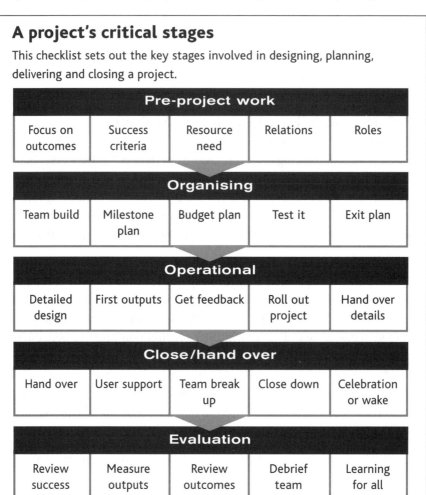

A project's critical stages

This checklist sets out the key stages involved in designing, planning, delivering and closing a project.

Pre-project work				
Focus on outcomes	Success criteria	Resource need	Relations	Roles

Organising				
Team build	Milestone plan	Budget plan	Test it	Exit plan

Operational				
Detailed design	First outputs	Get feedback	Roll out project	Hand over details

Close/hand over				
Hand over	User support	Team break up	Close down	Celebration or wake

Evaluation				
Review success	Measure outputs	Review outcomes	Debrief team	Learning for all

A pre-project phase

In this stage the project is still an idea. It needs to be defined and thought through. At the end of this stage a written project brief should be drafted setting out the key requirements, goals and resource requirements.

It is important in this stage to ensure that discussion is focused on what people want the project to achieve rather than what they want it to do. Focus on the 'ends' and not the 'means'. Project leaders need to probe the background to the project. What has created the need for it? How can we be sure that it is needed? It is worth trying to surface any hidden agendas – things that are either deliberately being overlooked or not being said.

Some techniques useful in this phase include:

Success criteria

Success criteria are statements of all of the factors that would make the project a success. They will include tangible factors and outputs such as the new structure being in place by the end of the year and outcome measures such as reduction in user complaints. Asking the question, 'For you, what will make this project a success?' to the project sponsor and other key stakeholders can be revealing and draws out useful goals and measures for the project.

Focus on the intended outcomes

Start at the end and then work to the means. An educational charity commissioned a project team to develop an intranet system so that they could share information amongst their members. The project team and sponsor produced an initial project brief that described the project in terms of technological outputs – what kind of computer system, what it would cost and what it would be able to do. After discussion they rejected it and drew up a project brief that described the intended benefits and gains to the organisation and its members in terms of what they would be able to do better. As one of the team commented, 'It would be easy to bring in a new IT system that met all the aspects of a typical technical specification, but did not make any difference to the organisation's performance and capacity. By setting out clear outcomes we have had to look at the whole picture and keep in our minds that the purpose of the project is to improve organisational communication and knowledge sharing – not just bringing in a computer system'.

Boundary setting

The process of delegating the project from the project sponsor to the project leader is about setting boundaries. The project leader needs to know how much independence and autonomy they have to run the project. It is possible to identify two boundaries:

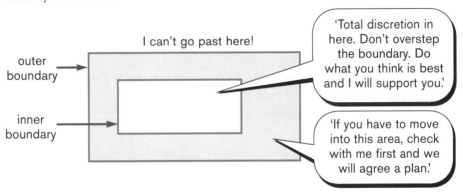

The area in the inner boundary is free for the project leader to operate in without having to seek approval of the project sponsor. The project leader can make decisions, carry out work and develop the project how s/he thinks fit – provided s/he does not step over the inner boundary. The outer boundary is the constraints on the project sponsor. The area between the inner and outer boundaries is one in which both parties should consult. The setting of the boundary might include discussion of several different issues:

Resources: 'You can spend up to £500 without reference to me.'
Organisational: 'You can allocate work to team members.'
External contacts: 'If you need to make contact with our major funders, talk to me first.'
Policy/political: 'All press releases must be cleared with me.'
Time: 'Organise how you like, but it must be ready by 20th November.'

Where to set the boundaries depends on a range of issues including the level of risk involved, the experience of the project leader, the organisational culture and the needs of the sponsor to be involved and feel in control. Boundary setting should be a clear and active task. If the boundaries are drawn too tight then the project leader might feel powerless as they to have to check everything with the sponsor. If the boundaries are drawn too wide the project leader might find such freedom threatening and feel a lack of support. Equally the project sponsor might find that such independence means that they become distant from the project and are not able to intervene quickly enough when there are problems.

It is important that both parties understand what has been delegated and how performance and progress will be reviewed. It is not uncommon in some organisations to only find out about the boundary once you have stepped over it. Some managers are very good at delegating work and jobs, but not so good at delegating decision-making power. They are happy to hand out work, but reluctant to hand out responsibility.

A project contract

One tool to bring this phase to a conclusion is to draft a simple project contract between the project sponsor and the project leader. This document should record the main terms of reference and goals for the project. It should record the following:

The success criteria for the project – intended outputs and outcomes
Resources allocated to the project
Issues delegated to the project leader
Key review dates

A project contract

This is an example of a *project contract* used by a development agency to set out responsibilities of a six month project to produce an agency-wide best practice manual.

PROJECT: BEST PRACTICE MANUAL

Project sponsor: Chief Executive.
Project Manager: Sue Jones – West Division.
Project Team: Alex Smith – HQ finance; Jo Bore – London Division;
    Ali Boss – Personnel.

■ Overall purpose of the project:

To produce an agency-wide manual setting out best practice for staff to follow in all core operations and tasks. The manual should develop best practice and assist in the implementation of an agency-wide quality assurance process.

■ Success criteria

▷ That a best practice manual is produced in time for launch at the staff conference in December.

▷ That operational staff have been fully involved in drawing up the manual and feedback indicates that they see it as a useful and supportive exercise.

▷ That the manual sets outs best practice in such a way that it can:
form a basis for quality standards acceptable to our main funders/purchasers
be used by supervisors in staff development and supervision.

▷ That service users are involved in identifying best practice and that feedback from the agency's user panel indicates that users have been involved.

▷ That the project is on budget and implementation of the manual does not involve any significant extra cost.

■ Resources assigned to the project

Expenses budget of £1500 Consultancy budget of £2000
Project Manager to spend no more than 20 days over 6 months on the project
Project team members to spend no more than 8 days over 6 months. Staff cover arrangements to be made locally. Requests for agency relief to be agreed by Chief Executive.

■ Project milestones:

▷ Structure of manual agreed – consultation document out to staff and users.
date: early August

▷ Best practice benchmarking groups in place. Estimated date: early September

▷ First drafts of practice standards ready. Estimated date: mid October

▷ Draft manual for consultation out to staff and user panels. Estimated date: late October

▷ Final draft to Agency Management Team for approval. Estimated date: mid-November

▷ Manual launched at staff conference. Estimated date: early December

Signed by Project Sponsor   Project Manager   Approved by Agency
      Management Team

The contract is a useful way of ensuring that the project is understood within the organisation and that the people know what it is intended to do. It also provides a key reference point in reviewing the project's progress and in evaluating success.

An organising/planning phase

Once the project has been defined, the project leader has several tasks that they must organise before the project can start.

Bringing the project team together

If the project has a team allocated to it then the project leader has a major task to ensure that the group starts to function as a team. Often at the start of a project people have been allocated to a project to represent or watch out for a particular interest. The leader of a team charged with creating a new organisational structure noted that 'it was frustrating at first. The accountant on the team was only interested in financial considerations and the case worker refused to acknowledge the management and resource implications of the project. It took a long time before people moved out of their traditional roles and saw the whole picture of the project'. The project leader needs to give some thought as to how to accelerate the process of moving the group from being a loose collection of individuals to a team with a strong sense of identity, direction and shared ownership. Teamwork is hard work. It needs time to develop and the planning of the project should take into account time needed to develop the team.

Ten quick ways to get a project team to start working well

1 Get each member to identify the skills and experience they can bring to the project. Encourage people to recognise the specific contribution that they can bring to the team.
2 Hold a special first team meeting to help the team to get to know each other and get to grips with the process. Consider using a skilled outside person to facilitate the meeting to ensure that the process works.
3 Spend time discussing the intended goals or outcomes of the project. Do not assume that people know what is expected or the background to the project.
4 Be prepared to vary the format of the discussion, e.g. small group work, devil's advocate and brainstorming to encourage a creative approach to the project.

---

5   Discuss and agree clear rules and standards of team behaviour –
    consider agreeing ground rules setting out how people should behave
    and work together.

6   Avoid jumping too quickly into the solution before discussing the
    problem or background to a problem. Get the team to explore the
    problem first. Make sure that they understand it.

7   Build in occasional review sessions to review how the team is working
    and see what can be improved.

8   Check that everyone accepts decisions: record them, display them and
    repeat them back. Make sure that action notes are circulated quickly.

9   Agree some immediate milestones and targets – a few early wins will
    make the team feel that they are making progress.

10 Try to ensure that everyone has a specific job or task to do after the
    first meeting. Commitment to the team comes from doing things for
    and with the team, not just by attending meetings.

Drawing up a project plan

A project needs a plan. Much of the literature on project management treats the
importance of project planning as if it were a precise and exact discipline. Often
project managers spend considerable time producing incredibly detailed plans
with schedules, critical paths and charts. The problem is that circumstances
change, events can not be predicted and humans have an ability to get in the way
of even the most organised plan. A project plan is needed that:

- identifies the key tasks needed
- makes people aware of what they must do and when
- gives an estimate of how long the project will take to complete
- allocates the project's budget and other resources
- allows for progress monitoring and identifies delays

A simple technique is to start at the end of the project and work backwards to
the beginning, identifying key milestones. A milestone is a point in the project's
life when one set of tasks has been completed and the project is ready to move
onto another stage. In some projects the milestones are fairly obvious. For
example, in buying and selling a house milestones might include: agreeing an
offer; agreeing a sale; arranging the mortgage; having surveys done; agreeing the
contract; and moving. To get to a milestone various tasks all have to be
completed. Building a project plan around milestones is a very useful team-
building exercise. It helps people working in the project understand it and see
how their role fits in to the project's success.

Planning how the project will close

Part of the plan needs to give thought to how the project will end and what will happen after the project has been wound up. Attention needs to be given to ensuring that people who may be involved in carrying the project on are involved and supported early. The idea of the invisible project team is very helpful here. Who are the people outside of the project team who will be important to the project continuing and being a success? How can they be involved? What support will they need?

A final check on feasibility

A final part of this phase is to check that the project team feels confident that the project can be done. Do people feel that they understand what is expected of them? Is the purpose of the project clear? Do they have the time, resources and relevant skills to do it? If the answer to these questions is mainly negative then further discussions are needed with the sponsor. It may be necessary to research the need and scope of the project further and do some sort of feasibility study, or it might be wise to scale the project down and do a pilot project to test and learn from it.

Operational phase

Up and running

When the project starts operating, the detailed design work starts. The project team need to spend time developing the content of their product, trying out new and creative ideas and shaping their plans. It is important that the project team does not become inward looking or lose sight of the original brief. The project leader has two main tasks: to keep the project focused, ensuring that it meets the brief and also to keep the rest of the organisation and others with an interest in the project informed and involved. Some strategies to do this include:

Use the milestones

The achievement of milestones helps the project team to feel that they are making progress. At the milestone it is worthwhile reviewing progress, checking that the project is on target and planning the detail of how to get to the next milestone. Getting to a milestone is an opportunity to raise the project's profile and let people know what progress has been made and what is planned to happen next.

Keep people 'wired in'

Project leaders need to ensure that key people know what the project is doing. Usually projects have a very high profile when they are first established and launched. However, sometimes people lose interest in them when they start doing the detailed work. Project leaders need to keep people informed, communicate progress and ensure that people are warned about any implications the project could have on their work.

Test ideas

A useful way of building up the invisible project team is to use them as a sounding board or reference group for the project team to try out their ideas and plans on. As well as providing useful and hopefully constructive feedback it might also help to manage change and identify potential problems.

Hand over or close down phase

The hand over phase of a project can be a difficult one. It is the point at which the product of the project (e.g. a new system, a reorganised service) is passed over from the project team to the people who have to live and work with it. It is about managing change and enabling the project to come to an end.

Hand over

The hand over needs to be a gradual process of rolling out the project and passing it over to the user. The invisible project team can be helpful in this. They can act as pilots, user representatives, coaches and examples of early users. The hand over needs to be planned. If it is rushed people may feel that the project has been 'dropped on them' and may become resistant to it.

User support

The project team needs to identify how it will support the user. What practical support can it give them? What new skills might users need? The learning process can help change provided it is not rushed and recognises the different ways in which people like to learn.

Team break up/close down

The project leader also needs to manage the break up of the project team. The project's end may represent a loss for some. It is important to help people to recognise what they have done and learnt during the project and celebrate their contribution to its success. To this end it's useful to try to end the project on a high point and acknowledge its achievements.

Evaluating the project

Often organisations overlook evaluation. They simply go onto the next project. Evaluation is an important exercise – it is really about organisational and individual learning and development. To do it well the aims and goals of the project need to be clear and have been recorded during the pre-project phase.

Review success

A good starting point is to ask the question, 'To what extent has the project been a success?' It is possible to answer this at different levels:

Tangible outputs	Did it produce and do the things that it said it would? Did it work to agreed specifications, time and budget?
Outcomes	Has it made a difference? What has changed or is changing?
Process	How did the project work? How did people feel about it?

Different people (users, project team members, the host and the sponsor) will probably have different views and inputs on these points.

Learning for all

It is useful to bring the project team back together to discuss the issues raised from the review of success. This can help to encourage individual and organisational learning. Questions to aid this process include:

What worked/what did not work ... why?

If we were doing this project again – with the benefit of hindsight – what would we do differently? What advice could you give?

What have you personally learnt from this project?

What new issues, side effects and needs have emerged as a result of this project?

The results of the evaluation should be shared, discussed and recorded within the organisation to ensure that future projects are stronger.

Why projects work

As part of their annual review and planning session the management team of a national agency looked at the different projects and task groups that the agency had had during the past year. Project teams had been set up to deliver a variety of initiatives including designing a new service, producing a quality standards document, and running a volunteer recruitment campaign. The management team recognised that some had worked well and others had failed. It decided to look at the ones that had worked and try to identify the factors and reasons why they had worked.

A clear champion

One common factor was that successful projects were led by an individual who was given and took real responsibility for the project's management and delivery. Often they had a high profile within the organisation – everyone knew that they were responsible for making it happen. They championed the project.

Strong sense of purpose

The projects that worked had written goals and purpose. Often they were called different things: mission, goals, objectives or aims. What they were called did not matter. What did matter was that the project team, the project sponsor and others connected to it had discussed, agreed and kept under review their purpose and relevance.

The project team had the right skills

How people came to be on project teams varied. Some teams were made up of people representing key interests within the organisation. Project team members often saw themselves as representing an interest or their bit of the organisation. Other teams were made up of people who were seen as having some spare time in their usual role. The projects that worked best were ones in which the project sponsor had clearly identified what sort of skills and knowledge expertise were needed at the start and then went out to recruit people who had a range of relevant skills to work on the team.

The project communicated

Several projects were criticised for being seen as secretive in how they worked. No one knew what the team were doing. They failed to keep people informed and often sprung surprises on people. One particular project was regarded as a success because of the way it involved and communicated with people outside of the project. The project team published a regular update news sheet, it held briefing meetings and developed a network of people inside and outside of the organisation to use as a sounding board for its ideas and also as a point to get feedback. This network, or invisible project team, proved to be essential in piloting the project's ideas and helping to anticipate and manage change.

A structured review process

For some projects there was a very deliberate and timed review and monitoring process. This stopped the project drifting or losing direction. It enabled progress to be discussed between the project sponsor and project leader. Blocks and barriers were identified and action taken. In other cases there were situations where projects had been allowed to run out of steam or get involved in issues that were irrelevant to them. A good review process helped to identify progress, recognise milestones and ensured that the project's profile was kept high.

chapter 7

CHANGE

Throughout this book we have looked at initiatives, strategies and factors that are intended to make organisations stronger, more effective and better able to respond to the world in which they operate. This final chapter looks at the process of bringing about change. All of the issues that we have looked at do require organisational change. But change is often fraught with difficulties. It can easily produce anxiety, resistance and conflicts. Many positive initiatives fail to materialise not because the idea behind the change or the proposal itself is faulty, but because the way it is introduced and managed fails. Even organisations which are about creating change in others can find change hard. A board member of a campaigning organisation described her experience of change in the following way:

'As a organisation we are all about campaigning and pressurising for change in society. We have some quite radical positions and push hard for change. However, internally it is very hard indeed to bring even the simplest change about. People cling to how things used to be. They are very reluctant to try new things out. The culture is stuck. It seems as if we are very good at demanding that others change, but not so good at changing ourselves.'

Types of change

All organisations experience different types of change. It is possible to group together types of organisational change into four main types:

Crisis or urgent change

This is imposed change. Events or circumstances mean that the organisation has to change if it is going to continue. Examples might include having to deal with a major funding cut or the departure of a key worker.

Reactive and responsive change

In this change people recognise that to continue, the organisation must respond to factors in the world outside. The organisation is responding to external events. Examples might include reacting to the impact of new legislation or to a new or emerging issue.

Strategic and planned change

This is proactive change. The organisation decides how it wants to develop and agrees a direction and future priorities. Strategic change usually requires the organisation to be different. Examples might include deciding to do more work with a particular client group or to move into a new geographical area.

Cultural and values change

Changes in culture and values are sometimes hard to identify. They involve changing the prevailing style, attitude and organisational 'common sense'. Cultural change examples include altering how an organisation treats its users or encouraging local managers to make decisions without constant reference back to their seniors.

All of these types of changes can connect up. If an organisation does not react quickly enough then it may have to deal with a crisis. Often organisations start working on strategic planning and strategic management to avoid spending all their time simply reacting or dealing with crisis. For a new strategy to be successful, a change in culture and how the organisation operates is needed. Here are some of the issues relevant to dealing with these types of change:

Crisis or urgent change

Features: Often the issue is thrown at the organisation and it has to be dealt with quickly. The issue can produce a feeling of being out of control or panic.

Approaches: Managers must take control of the issue and identify the difference between what is urgent and what is important. Managers must not avoid the issue, but ensure that it is dealt with in a rational and level-headed way. In responding to the change it is important to explore all of the options open and not choose a 'quick fix' or something that might delay the issue, but not deal with it.

Dangers: Some managers and organisations have a style which means that they only act when something becomes a crisis. In a crisis situation communication often gets harder as people need to act quickly. Some managers have been known to welcome a crisis situation (or threat of) as it gives them a reason to push through other reforms and changes that in 'normal' circumstances would not be acceptable.

Reactive and responsive change

Features: The organisation needs to be able to spot the issues in its external environment early enough for it to react in a planned and thoughtful way rather than in a panic. Failure to act can lead to a crisis. Managers must exercise a political judgment about which issues are critical ones and will need a significant response.

Approaches: Managers need to develop good antennae that can help them to spot potential trends and factors that will necessitate change. They also need to encourage staff who work at the 'sharp end', the boundary between the organisation and its users, to identify new and emerging trends and report them back.

Dangers: Often people are so busy working (or just not interested) that they fail to see issues or recognise their impact on the organisation. They only see problems when it is too late.

Strategic and planned change

Features: In strategic or planned change the organisation makes choices about how it wants to develop and position itself. This usually happens after some sort of planning process.

Approaches: Managers have to ensure that a process is used which enables people in the organisation to contribute to and participate in the discussions, debates and decisions that produce the strategy. People need to feel that they understand the direction and can relate their work to it. The strategy must be expressed in terms that 'make it real' for people – they can understand how the organisation intends to develop and can see the implications for them.

Dangers: Managers have to be careful that they do not stick too rigidly to the plan. It needs to be reviewed and updated. The strategy needs to be a practical process. It needs to make clear what the first steps are, how it will be resourced and how it will be measured. Failure to do this will mean that the strategy lacks any credibility or practical relevance.

Cultural and values change

Features: Cultural change is about changing the values, attitudes and outlooks that are played out in the organisation's day-to-day work. Culture can be hard to define or different cultures can exist in different parts of the organisation. What makes up an organisation's culture can be deeply ingrained. It comes from history, past experience and traditions.

Approaches: It is usually more effective to focus on behaviours than on beliefs. Managers should identify the cultures by highlighting their impact on what the organisation does and delivers. Often managers need to take the lead in describing how they see the current culture, its impact and then how they would like to see it change. Managers as individuals must be prepared to change their behaviour and actions first. People watch for clues.

Dangers: Often we underestimate how fixed a culture is. Sometimes people adjust to a new style of working (e.g. by using a new set of in buzz words) and give the appearance of change, but at the first opportunity they revert back to the practices and ways of doing things of the old culture.

Culture at work

A group of public and voluntary sector managers produced a list of statements that described dominant cultures at work. See if you recognise any:

1 **'It's not my job'**
   Staff only take responsibility for their job or areas of responsibility. If something is outside of their remit they do not feel responsible to ensure that the users is dealt with. Often users get passed around the organisation until they give up trying to find out who is responsible.

2 **'We know best about your problem'**
   Staff have seen it all before and know what the user experiences, needs and wants probably better than what they do. They see little point in finding out what users want as they have years and years of experience.

3 **'Wait until it becomes urgent or a crisis'**
   The organisation only acts when it has to. There is always an uncertainty about planning or change so it is best to sit it out and wait to see what happens.

4 **'Cover your back'**
   Any decision, however minor, is passed up the line. Staff have views and opinions but are reluctant to take personal responsibility for decisions. They feel safer if the decision to do something is made or approved by someone senior.

5 **'We must be effective ... we are growing'**
   The fact that the organisation is growing must mean that it is effective and doing the right thing. Expansion, growth and increase in volume must be good. All the measures that matter are quantitative.

6 **'It's always xyz's fault ... '**
   A blame culture. Problems are always caused by the funding body or headquarters or the management committee or another team colleague. Time is spent allocating blame rather than solving or preventing problems.

Discussion:

What statements sum up the culture (or sub cultures) that operate in your organisation or workplace?
What factors contribute to or shape this culture?
In what ways would you like the culture to change?
What might be the first steps in doing this?

Managing through change

Introducing and managing change in a workplace does need careful thought and some planning. Managers need to think through the process for managing change. They need to be able to identify blocks and barriers to the change and spot concerns and potential obstructions. They also need to perform a balancing act. On one side they have a responsibility to their organisation to ensure that the change takes place, that progress is made and that plans are kept to. On the other hand they also have a responsibility to their staff. They need to give people time to get used to the change, overcome anxieties and adapt to new roles and expectations. Often this can create a conflict and leaves the manager feeling squeezed.

A useful model or thinking tool for understanding what happens to people in a period of change was presented by Flora and Elkind. They suggest that people move through four stages:

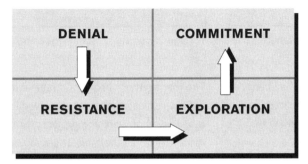

In the **denial** stage, people's reaction might include:

'It will never happen'
'It doesn't really mean anything to me'

Often people decide not to engage in the change initiative. They opt out or switch off from discussions. They might believe that if they keep their heads down, the change will go away.

The **resistance** stage might take a number of different forms. Active resistance could include conflicts, industrial relations disputes and vocal arguments between staff and managers. Passive resistance can include people not engaging in discussions and not participating in anything connected to the change.

The **exploration** stage might be a gradual one. People slowly start to consider the issues involved in the change and start to find out more about it. They start to find their own way through some of the confusion. They start to experiment and test out the change idea.

In the **commitment** stage people start to adjust to and incorporate the change. They learn new ways of working and start to feel a sense of being in charge for the detail, implementation and organisation of the change itself.

Managing change – a question of style

Managers have a choice about how to introduce, lead and manage change. This box sets out four different positions that managers can adopt in managing change – ranging from a top down direction to managing through trying to achieve a shared consensus.

Position 1: Top down direction	Position 2: Chance to input
'I am in charge ... here's what is going to happen ...'	*'I will make the decision about what to do, anyone with any input can talk to me ...'*
Managers discuss, decide and inform others of the details of change. Managers control the direction and take responsibility for all decisions.	Before making a decision on how to change, those with power ask people for their views.

manager's control ▨	staff involvement ☐	manager's control ▨	staff involvement ☐

The newly appointed Director of a charity realised that the fundraising department was failing to reach its targets. She knew that her predecessor had tried to influence a change in strategy, but had met with delays, staff resistance and requests for consultation. She called a staff meeting, explained the new strategy and gave each staff member a briefing note on how it would affect them and their personal targets.	The management board of a regeneration agency realised that it was involved in too many areas of work and projects for the resources it had available. It quickly needed to review its strategy. The board decided to delay a decision for three weeks and to write to all its staff and key partners to ask them for their views. Several people responded and when the board convened it had a summary of staff views.

All of the positions have advantages and disadvantages. Key factors in determining which position to adopt might include:

The nature of the change

The level of risk involved, the different impact on individuals, and the time available for discussion all need to be considered. Trying to consult or develop a consensus over a negative or threatening change such as how to handle the need for redundancies within a team would probably be unproductive. Managers may have to be prepared to be more directive in dealing with such a change.

The importance of involvement

The earlier that people are involved in discussing and planning the change could lead to greater involvement and sense of ownership and responsibility for the change. A consensus style of management might create a commitment to work on the change.

Position 3: Active consultation

'Here are the issues and options facing us ... what do you think we should do?'

People should be consulted in times of change. People need time to consider the issues and express their views.

manager's control ■   staff involvement □

The Director of a housing association knew that their current organisational structure did not work. He circulated a paper setting out how he saw the problem and suggesting options for change. Staff met in teams to discuss the issue and then fed back comments and alternative options. He then prepared recommendations for the management board.

Position 4: Shared consensus

'This is the problem, we are all in it together, so let's get a consensus about what to do'

When faced with significant change managers should get a consensus. They should facilitate the process to find a solution that has support.

manager's control ■   staff involvement □

Faced with a downturn in income, the staff team of a training agency met for a day to agree how to proceed. The staff team worked together to come up with a future strategy and make revisions to the budget. The agency's manager worked to ensure that a solution was reached that everyone 'owned' and met the criteria agreed by the agency's trustees.

The style and culture of the organisation

Managers need to understand the culture and style of their organisation. It is hard to be a democratic and participatory manager when you are managed by dictatorial zealots.

The opportunity for input and involvement

In some change situations there is little room for manoeuvre. The opportunity to influence the change is small. To pretend otherwise will probably backfire and create cynicism and conflict.

It is important that managers are open and clear about what level of involvement and consultation is available to staff in a change process and let staff know when and how they can contribute to the process.

Managers can do a lot to help people through this transitional period. The journey through it can be a difficult and strenuous one and some changes get blocked early on and never move forward. Or it can be a positive and learning experience. Here are ten things that managers can do to help people through this transition grid:

1 **Focus on why**

   Do not assume that people see the reasons for the change taking place. Managers may need to spend time helping people to see the broader context that creates the need for change. One housing agency had to run an internal education programme with seminars and visits to other agencies to explain the background to the changes being demanded by their main funder. The agency's coordinator was surprised at how little some staff knew about changes in government policy direction, 'We had to help people through a fast learning curve, before we could get people to consider the implications of the change'.

2 **See the change as building on and not demolishing the past**

   A common mistake managers make in introducing change is to imply that the new order will be brilliant and flawless and that all that has gone before was poor and ineffective. The new director of a charity introduced a quality assurance initiative in such a way that staff felt that it was implied that the organisation lacked quality. They felt defensive and hostile. Their perception was that the Director was saying that quality work was 'new' and had been lacking in the past. An alternative approach would be to see the change to a quality assurance as building on and adding to existing good practice.

3 **Don't write people off**

   Some people may have a first reaction to change that is negative, resistant and opposed. Managers need to handle resistance carefully. If they respond severely to any initial objections to the change they may run the risk of closing down discussion and dialogue. Faced with resistance managers need to spend time getting informed discussions going, letting people express feelings of anxiety and helping people to see how they can influence how the change is implemented. The alternative is to retreat, become distant and remote in communication and thereby become isolated.

4 **Manage time**

   People do need time to work through the stages of denial, resistance, exploration and commitment. It is worthwhile to plan out and publish the time available for consultation and discussion and also the timetable for making decisions to prevent the process dragging out. In most situations the earlier that people are involved the better.

5 **Be honest and open**

If, in a period of change, managers try to keep relevant information secret and private it will create a climate of suspicion and mistrust. Some factors such as individual personnel issues or the detailed issues involved in some negotiations may need to be treated as confidential. However, managers should encourage access to information and as a matter of principle be honest about what they know and think.

6 **Create structures for dialogue**

In some organisations it is necessary to create the structures and systems for communication and involvement. These may take the form of regular staff meetings, individual one-to-one meetings or formal negotiating structures with recognised trade unions and other consultative forums. When such structures work they provide a channel for people to express their concerns and to make a managed input into the change process. They can also take the sting out of conflicts by providing a formal process for conflicts to be resolved.

7 **Be available**

Managers need to be available and accessible during periods of change. This is particularly important if staff feel that they are likely to be badly affected by the change. Managers must avoid a defensive tendency to hide during difficult times by always being busy and not available.

8 **Create learning and support**

Relevant learning can help people face up to and respond to change. Managers need to ensure that different forms of learning are available throughout the change process. Good organised learning can make people feel able and confident to deal with the change.

9 **Spot side effects**

Organisational change usually creates side effects. These can be hard to predict at the start, but managers need to look out for them and ensure that they are dealt with. Spin-off effects include new skills being needed, systems needing to change, pay and grading issues and the need to update rules and procedures. Often a failure to deal with side effects will block change.

10 **Highlight early success**

One strategy is to look for early examples of the change working. When examples are found they can be shared and celebrated. They can also provide a useful confidence boost and help other people to see the change as real.

Using learning to support change

Learning has a key role in introducing, supporting and helping people to change. It needs to be a continual process and not simply a one-off.

One employee of a national charity described how not to do it:

> 'Whenever there is a change afoot my organisation has what we call a "sheep dip" approach to learning. A training course is put in that everyone has to attend. The organisation feels good because everyone has been through it but it is pure chance if it is relevant to you, at the right level and at the right time.'

Here are some examples of the kinds of things that organisations can do to encourage learning at work:

Action learning sets: A small group of people meeting together on a regular basis to share and work on real life issues. Participants get support and gain insight by asking questions and helping group members work on their issues.

Coaching: One-to-one support, tuition and feedback to help people develop new skills and abilities.

Distance learning material: Prepared written material such as case studies, text, practical exercises.

Evaluation studies: Evaluation is about looking at a piece of work, project or activity to see if it is achieving its original aims, gathering information and data on its performance and success, and identifying new needs and objectives.

Job shadowing: Observing a colleague at work to gain an insight into the skills, approach and knowledge involved.

Job swaps: A temporary exchange of jobs and roles, often following on from a job shadowing exercise.

Mentors: An experienced person acts as a contact point for someone in a new role or learning a new skill. The mentor provides coaching, support, advice and acts as a sounding board.

Observation: By watching and analysing a piece of work in progress, the observer gains an insight into it that can help them to develop.

Pilot projects: A pilot project is an attempt to test the ideas and assumptions behind a bigger initiative or project. As well as seeing if the project works it is a useful way of identifying and developing new skills.

Research projects: Time away from work to do desk research and other formal research techniques to find out more about an issue, its background and best practice.

Resource banks: The organisation puts together relevant materials such as books, press cuttings and past examples so that staff have an in-house body of expertise to consult.

Secondments: Temporary secondment to another organisation or team which has particular skills, expertise or recent experience of similar issues.

Simulations: A dummy run. A new system is tested by running a made-up example to test the new system and give people an experience of it.

Task forces/projects groups: By introducing the change through task and project groups, people learn from the process and from each other.

Technology-based training: The use of computer-based learning, CD-ROMS and the internet.

USING A FORCE FIELD ANALYSIS TO ASSESS AND PLAN CHANGE

This well-established technique is a very quick way to analyse and plan change. It consists of four elements:

▶ **The current state:** the status quo and current situation.
▶ **The desired state:** the vision of how we want things to be.
▶ **Restraining forces:** factors and arguments working against the change.
▶ **Driving forces:** factors and argument working for the change.

This example is one produced by a manager of a Health Development Agency who wanted to move away from a central office to three local offices.

The technique helps to organise negotiating arguments, identify points of influence and helps to monitor the change as it develops.

DESIRED STATE:
Staff working in three local offices – providing a multi-skilled service to our users

Restraining forces working against change

- Pay structure rewards 'specialists' not 'generalists'
- Who will support local staff?
- Financial costs of moving to 3 local offices
- Some staff feel multi-skilled work reduces their professional status
- Some staff threatened by multi-skilled work

CURRENT STATE:
Staff operate in four service teams – all based at head office – not very accessible – lack of a joined up service thinking

Driving forces working for change

- Main funders back the idea
- New pay policy will reward multi-skilled working
- Comprehensive training programme to be set up
- Pilot scheme was very successful
- Expert help desk and intranet to be established
- Central office costs very high and likely to rise
- Strong support from users and trustees for local offices

A change that worked

Nashville Youth Agency is an independent agency working with young people in the Borough of Nashville. It employs twenty-six full-time staff and over 100 part-time and sessional staff. Staff provide a range of services and activities for young people in youth centres, detached work and other projects throughout Nashville.

Two years ago Val, the agency's Director felt a strong need to reorganise the agency. She felt that service practices ranged from poor to brilliant, that the agency's management systems and structures were creaking and that many staff failed to see themselves as being part of a one agency – they related to their centre or project, but not to the agency as a whole. Val knew that if she simply announced changes they would blocked so she set about designing a process to introduce and bring about change.

After discussions with her two assistant directors and management committee, Val organised a one-day conference on the future of the agency. The day was attended by nearly all full-time staff, representatives of part-time staff, most of the management committee and invited 'experts' including an academic who specialised in youth work, two representatives from the agency's main funders and four young people who used the agency's services.

The day started with presentations looking at the changing nature of young people's experience and ideas on how the agency could develop. Val gave a candid appraisal of how she saw the agency and the choices open to it. People worked in groups to discuss the issues and to plan out how the agency could develop. In the final session a list was produced of 'how things are now and how they could be':

Current state How they are now	Future state How we want them to be
Lots of good work and lots of not so good work – practice varies	Consistent quality work across the agency
Management seen as remote, centralised and unhelpful	Management adds value – it is in touch with and supports delivery
Sessional staff don't feel part of the whole agency	Staff feel part of a positive and valuable team
Not many career or development opportunities	We are a learning organisation

At the end of the day Val asked for volunteers to work with her to develop ideas on how to get from the current state to the future state. A group of staff and committee members were asked to meet three times and report back to the organisation and then produce recommendations for the management committee.

The group, named the 'change team', met quickly after the event and brainstormed ideas. Before their second meeting members of the group went off to visit other similar agencies to gain a comparison (or to steal their ideas as one person put it).

After the second meeting a three-page document called Proposal for Change was drawn up by Val as Director in consultation with group members. It summarised the discussion at the conference and made three main proposals:

1   That the agency produce a quality standards framework setting out the best practice to be followed across all centres and projects.

2   That the management structure be reorganised (at no extra cost) to create four area managers responsible for all services in a geographical patch.

3   That staff be encouraged to work across centres and projects and not just in one centre's project.

It was quickly recognised that the changes could have some negative issues for some staff. At least one of the assistant director posts could go and some centre manager posts would be redeployed into the new area manager posts. Some staff perceived the introduction of area managers and the push to regulate quality and practice as being an attempt by the head office to control and direct local workers.

Val got the management committee to agree to a set of principles about how the change would be managed. These included maximum open communication and information, active consultation and an agreement with the staff trade union on how any job reorganisation, redeployment or potential redundancy would be handled.

For the next three months the organisation embarked on a process of implementing the changes:

Three staff groups were set up to work on different aspects of quality standards. They were charged with the responsibility of identifying best practice in the agency and recording them as quality standards.

A group of committee members and Val worked to redesign the management structure, work out how it could be costed and the process by which the change could be managed.

The management team met to see how staff could be encouraged to work across centres. To test the idea a pilot work shadowing scheme was run between three projects.

Throughout the process Val produced a fortnightly news bulletin circulated to all staff and committee members. Open forums were held throughout the agency where staff members could ask questions, express concerns and feed into the process. Val and the Chair of the committee also made time to 'be around' the agency more to talk and listen to staff.

At the end of the three months the working parties reported. The draft quality standards still needed some more work, but were generally seen as being positive by staff and funders. A system for managing staff transfers, secondments and joint working was also agreed. A new management structure was agreed and a procedure for redeploying staff was agreed.

There was some opposition, animosity and anxiety around the proposals. Discussions, consultation and negotiations did lead to some amendments and changes to the proposals that the management committee agreed to. The implementation of the change did take time. Two managers left the organisation, but after an open recruitment process the new structure was in place.

The changes have helped the agency to overcome many of the issues Val identified at the start of the process.

Lessons learnt

Val could identify six main learning points from this experience:

1 **Don't lose the big picture**

    Managers should never assume that people know, understand or appreciate the context or reasons why change is necessary. At Nashville time was spent trying to get a consensus about what sort of organisation we wanted to be. This took time, but was worthwhile.

2 **Communicate like never before**

    In a period of change managers need to work as fast as the organisational grapevine. Bulletins, briefings, staff meetings and other forms of communication can all be used to update people, inform and involve. No one communication technique works all of the time. It is easy for managers to retreat and hide away during difficult times, but it is critical that managers are visible and accessible to people to hear and discuss their concerns.

3 **Change is a personal thing**
People react differently and at different times. Some are quick to be involved, others take time. Some see threats and others see opportunities. People need time to see the issues, consider the intended change and work out the implications. Do not write people off who are not enthusiastic from day one.

4 **Manage time**
People want time for consultation, discussion and debate. However, a badly managed consultation process can just drag on and on until the issue dies. At Nashville strict timescales were set for consultation. There comes a point when consultation has to end and decisions have to be made. If managers miss that point then the momentum for change may be lost.

5 **Be clear about the process**
Nashville agency was very clear about when, how and by whom decisions would be made. The process and timetable for planning and considering the change needs to be open and understood. People need to know how any difficult decisions will be made and, where possible, that there are fair and objective criteria for making them.

6 **Ownership creates progress**
Val could probably have come up with the reorganisation plan and the quality standards much quicker by working on her own, without setting up groups and having away days and so on. The experience at Nashville suggested that involving staff in task groups and in producing ideas helped people to learn, ensured that ideas were practical, but most of all led to a feeling that the change came from the organisation rather than 'being done to them'.

'There is nothing more difficult to plan, more doubtful of success, nor more dangerous to manage than the creation of a new system.

'For the initiator has the active enmity of all who would profit by the preservation of the old system and merely lukewarm defenders in those who would gain by the new one.'

Machiavelli
The Prince

RESOURCES

Using a consultant

Often when organisations are at a critical point in their development they turn to a consultant to help them. Consultants come in all shapes and sizes ranging from individuals operating on a freelance basis to large companies.

Typical reasons to use a consultant

1   **When there is a definite knowledge gap**
    A consultant may be used to develop the organisation's capacity in an expert area such as information technology, marketing or fundraising. As well as doing a job or solving a problem the consultancy should leave the organisation stronger and more skilled.

2   **When an issue or decision in the organisation is blocked and is unable to be resolved**
    Consultants can be used to facilitate a process. The consultant should take no part in nor have any view on the content of the decision, but should have skills to help the organisation make progress on an issue that has been blocking them. The consultant needs to have strong facilitation skills and be able to help people reach an effective solution.

3   **When an objective perspective is needed**
    Consultants are often used to review an issue or to help test out an idea. They should bring an experienced and independent view that will help in evaluating progress or making future decisions.

4   **To bring credibility**
    Sometimes consultants are used to make potential or existing funders feel confident that their investment is in safe hands. The consultant might prepare a report reviewing the organisation or provide support and advice to the organisation's staff and board.

Good practice about consultancy

1   **Be specific**
    Before engaging a consultant ensure that your organisation knows exactly why it is bringing in an external person or agency. What special insight, skill or expertise do you need them to have? Think about the outcomes of the exercise – when the consultancy has finished what will you want to be different? It is probably better to be specific about what you want the consultant to bring about or deliver rather than what the consultant will do.

2   **Spend time on recruitment**

It is worthwhile to write a short brief for the consultancy setting out what you want it to achieve. The brief should be circulated to several consultants who should be asked to submit a tender for it. You should ask them to describe how they would approach the issues listed in the brief, their experience of similar projects and the cost and timescale for the project. It is worth checking who will actually do the work. Larger firms have been criticised for using their most experienced and impressive consultants to bid for work, as once the firm is appointed the work is then passed onto more junior and less experienced staff.

3   **Write an agreement**

When you have decided who to appoint it is sensible to issue a simple agreement setting out the arrangement and clarifying expectations. The agreement should include:

- Purpose of the consultancy
- Specific tasks to be carried out
- Who the consultant will report to
- Timescale for the work
- Specific requirements – respecting confidentiality or equal opportunities
- Fee – including expenses and payment schedule
- Ownership/copyright of any material produced
- Review arrangements

Seemingly straightforward issues such as to whom the consultant reports need to be clarified and agreed at the start.

4   **Let the consultant get to know you**

Ensure that the consultant has the chance to fully understand the background, structures, culture and style of your organisation. Their ideas and recommendations need to fit with your organisation.

5   **Go from analysis to action**

Often consultants can be criticised for delivering an impressive looking written report that identifies problems and makes sensible recommendations. The consultant disappears when the hard work of implementing the recommendations starts. Ensure that the consultant will be available for support and involvement in the implementation stage.

6   **Don't become dependent on a consultant**

A consultancy should be a learning process – the organisation should emerge from it stronger. Good consultants are skilled at working their way out of the organisation and leaving it able to do or follow through on the issues that the consultancy was needed to address. If you are unable to operate without long-term support from the consultant then the process and style of the consultancy needs reviewing.

7   **Review progress**
Build into the process occasional review meetings to evaluate progress against that brief.

Information about consultants

There are two main lists of consultants specialising in not for profit organisations:

The Management Development Network publishes a directory of voluntary sector management consultants and trainers.

Management Development Network
c/o 39 Gabriel House,
10 Odessa Street
London SE16 7HQ
tel 020 7232 0726
fax 020 7237 8117
e-mail mdn@sandy-a.dircon.co.uk

The National Council for Voluntary Organisations keeps an approved list of consultants who have passed through a quality assurance process.

National Council for Voluntary Organisations
Regent's Wharf
8 All Saints Street
London N1 9RL
tel 020 7713 6161
fax 020 7713 6300

FURTHER READING

Titles in this list published by the Directory of Social Change are available from DSC Books, 24 Stephenson Way, London NW1 2DP. Call 020 7209 5151 for a free publications list. Prices were correct at time of going to press, but may be subject to change.

The Complete Guide to Business & Strategic Planning
Alan Lawrie, 1994. Price £10.95
ISBN 1 873860 61 7 Directory of Social Change

The Complete Guide to Creating and Managing New Projects
Alan Lawrie, 1996. Price £12.50
ISBN 1 873860 91 9 Directory of Social Change

Designing Organisations
Philip Sanders, 1994. Price £16.95
ISBN 0 7494 1394 8 Kogan Page

The Fifth Discipline Fieldbook
Peter Senge et al, 1999. Price £19.99
ISBN 1 85788 060 9 Nicholas Brealey Publishing

Managing Conflict
Gill Taylor, 1999. Price £12.50
ISBN 1 900360 28 4 Directory of Social Change

Managing Organisational Change
Cynthia Scott & Dennis T. Jaffe, 1989. Price £7.99
ISBN 0 7494 0102 8 Kogan Page

Managing People
Gill Taylor & Christine Thornton, 1995. Price £10.95
ISBN 1 873860471 Directory of Social Change

Managing Quality of Service
Alan Lawrie, 1995. Price £10.95
ISBN 1 873860 86 2 Directory of Social Change

Managing Without Profit
Mike Hudson, 1999. Price £12.99
ISBN 0 14 023886 7 Penguin, available from DSC

Project Leadership
Wendy Briner, Michael Geddes & Colin Hastings, 1996. Price £16.95
ISBN 0 556 02794 1 Gower Publishing